Guitar Fretboard Memorization

A comprehensive guide to knowing the neck

by Tom Fleming

ISBN 978-1-5400-6859-0

Visit Hal Leonard Online at
www.halleonard.com

Contact us:
Hal Leonard
7777 West Bluemound Road
Milwaukee, WI 53213
Email: info@halleonard.com

In Europe, contact:
Hal Leonard Europe Limited
42 Wigmore Street
Marylebone, London, W1U 2RN
Email: info@halleonardeurope.com

In Australia, contact:
Hal Leonard Australia Pty. Ltd.
4 Lentara Court
Cheltenham, Victoria, 3192 Australia
Email: info@halleonard.com.au

CONTENTS

Introduction 4

Chapter 1: Getting Started. 5

Chapter 2: The Chromatic Scale and Diatonic Movement. 13

Chapter 3: Understanding Key Signatures and Enharmonics 21

Chapter 4: Introducing Intervals. 24

Chapter 5: Exploring the Major Scale 32

Chapter 6: Pentatonic Scales 40

Chapter 7: Melodic and Harmonic Minor Scales 44

Chapter 8: The Blues Scale. 49

Chapter 9: First-Position Chords 53

Chapter 10: Triads 57

Chapter 11: Arpeggios and Other Chord Shapes 68

Chapter 12: More Scale Fingerings 76

Chapter 13: Joining the Dots with Fretboard Mapping. 89

INTRODUCTION

Learning to play the guitar, perhaps more than any other instrument, can be a highly fragmented business. Ask any great guitar player, and you will find that they didn't simply go to one teacher for years or use one general-purpose method book. Most people have studied formally or informally with teachers and friends, used any number of books, and augmented their learning with a plethora of DVDs, online courses, YouTube channels, and other resources. Many people have also spent a large amount of time listening to—and perhaps attempting to transcribe—their favorite players' signature ideas.

There's a great deal to be mastered along the way, from the basic mechanics of playing through a world of technique, chord vocabulary, scale knowledge, harmonic knowledge and music, theory, styles, guitar and amp tones... the list of learning opportunities is endless!

This book does not directly address all of these things; there are plenty of teachers, books, and other resources for that. Instead, it attempts to address one of the drawbacks of this fragmentation and of the guitar itself: There has never been a straightforward path to *knowing where everything is*. Many aspects of guitar playing, from sight reading to improvising, are made so much harder because many notes can be found in several different places. On a keyboard instrument, any given note can only be found in one place. On the guitar, you may know the note you'd like to play, whether you are reading or improvising, but can you find it in the fretboard area where you have happened to land? If you choose one location of a particular note, will you run into problems later in the phrase?

The goal of this book is to help the reader ease these issues and work towards a secure understanding of the way the guitar fretboard works—in simple terms, a path to being able to find any note, scale, or chord anywhere on the neck.

CHAPTER 1: GETTING STARTED

Using Fretboard Markers

Most guitars have fretboard markers (dots, blocks, or other inlays) placed at various locations. These can be very helpful for locating notes and establishing an over-all sense of fretboard geography.

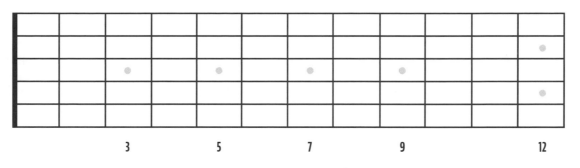

Modern guitars generally have markers at frets 3, 5, 7, 9, and 12; a marker may occasionally be found at fret 1. Of course, some guitars have no markers at all—in which case, you may want to use small, removable stickers as temporary aids while working through this book. Because the 12th fret is an octave above the open string, the note names repeat from there.

In our quest to memorize the entire guitar fretboard and all the resources you might want to play on it, we have to start somewhere. Let's begin with the names of the open strings.

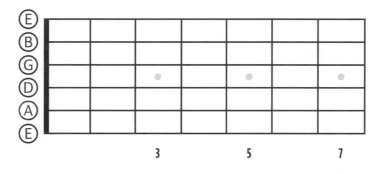

You'll see many mnemonic devices suggested as a way to memorize the names of the open strings, such as, "**E**very **A**mateur **D**oes **G**et **B**etter **E**ventually." We suggest coming up with your own device—a personal phrase is likely to be more memorable.

The open strings are shown in guitar tablature as zeros. Fretted notes are represented by higher numbers corresponding to the fret in use.

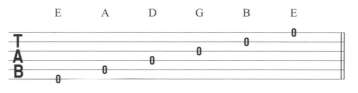

In standard notation, the notes E, A, D, G, B, and E are shown like this:

In guitar music, standard notation and tablature are usually shown together.

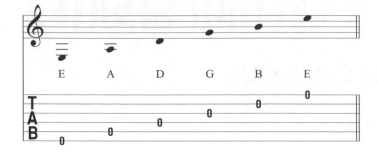

Exercise

Create your own mnemonic device for the names of the open strings in either direction (E–A–D–G–B–E or E–B–G–D–A–E) or both.

The Natural Notes: C Major

Along with the open strings, the first four frets of the guitar—also known as **1st position**—are key to learning the entire fretboard. Let's begin with the **natural** notes, which correspond to the white keys on a piano and are named using the first seven letters of the alphabet. Here are all the natural notes found in 1st position:

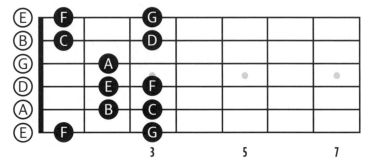

Clearly, this is too much information to digest at once. The best way to begin to assimilate these notes is to play them as a scale and say each note as it is played. These natural notes, when played starting and finishing with the note C, are known as the **C major scale**.

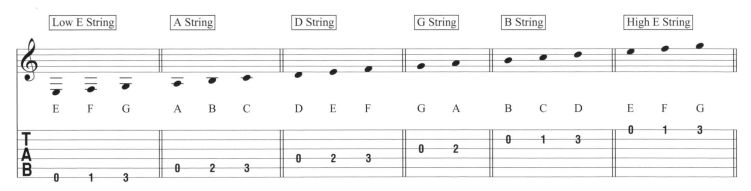

The most complete and consistent way to learn scales is to start with the lowest available **tonic note** (the note giving the scale its name, in this case, "C"), ascend to the highest note in the given position or fretboard area, down to the lowest available note, and finally back up to the tonic/starting note.

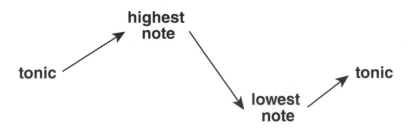

Here's the C major scale laid out in this way:

Exercise

Play the C major scale as shown in the previous notated example, saying the note names out loud until you have it memorized.

Tip: While we are not focusing on guitar technique here, if you are practicing scales, then you may as well be doing it in a productive way that benefits your playing overall. We recommend always playing 1st position scales using one finger per fret (first finger always plays the first fret, second finger plays the second fret, and so on) and using **alternate picking** (continuous down/up picking, feeling the downstrokes as falling on the beat).

Sharps and Flats

The notes in between the natural notes are known as **sharps** and **flats**, and they correspond to the black notes on the piano. Think of **sharp** as meaning "higher than" while **flat** means "lower than." So the note between F and G (for example, the 2nd fret of either E string) can be called either F-sharp (F♯) or G-flat (G♭), depending on the context. When you move consecutively between flat, sharps, and naturals from one fret to the next, you're moving in increments of **half tones** (also called **half steps**).

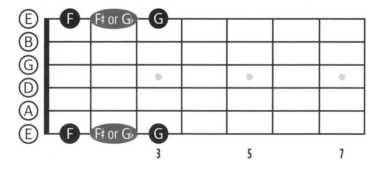

After the C major scale, we need just a few additional scales to integrate all of the sharps and flats in 1st position.

A Harmonic Minor (Introducing G♯)

The **A harmonic minor scale** uses the same notes as C major, with one exception: the note G is raised to G♯. Also, instead of starting and ending on C, we start and end on A. Because of this relationship to C major, A minor is known as the **relative minor** of C major. (We will discuss the harmonic minor scale and others in greater depth in later chapters.) There are three G♯ notes in 1st position.

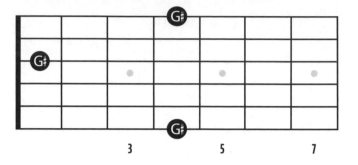

Here's the full A harmonic minor scale in 1st position (the tonic notes are indicated with a square):

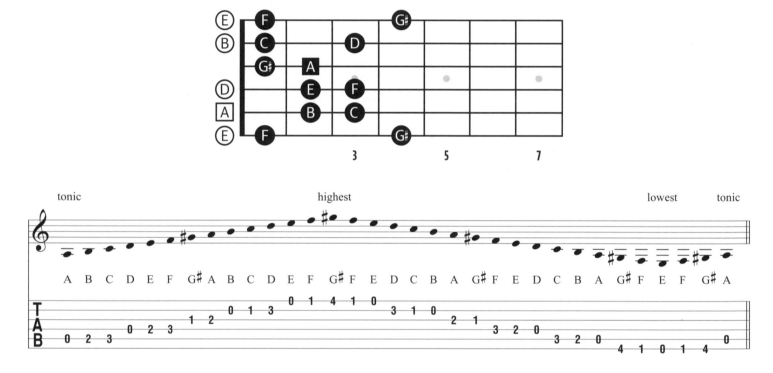

Exercise

Play the A harmonic minor scale as shown in the previous example, saying the note names out loud until you have it memorized.

Tip: The note G♯ can also be called A♭ in other contexts.

G Major (Introducing F#)

The G major scale is mostly constructed from natural notes, with the exception of the note F#. There are three different F# notes in 1st position.

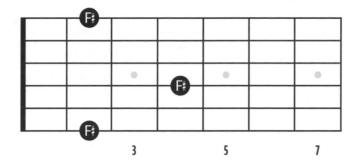

Here is the G major scale in 1st position:

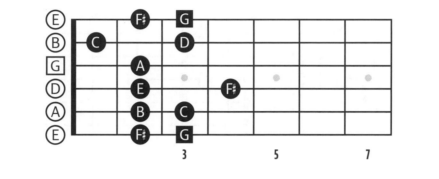

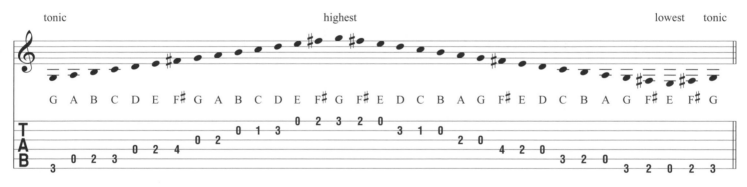

Exercise

Play the G major scale as shown in the previous example, saying the note names out loud until you have it memorized.

Tip: The note F# can also be called G♭ in other contexts.

E Harmonic Minor (Introducing D#)

E minor is the relative minor of G major. This means that the E harmonic minor scale shares the notes of G major, with one exception: D is raised to D#. So the notes of E harmonic minor are E, F#, G, A, B, C, and D#. There are only two D# notes in 1st position.

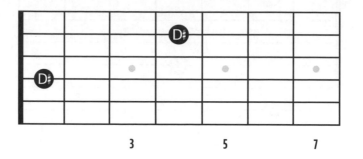

Here is the E harmonic minor scale in 1st position:

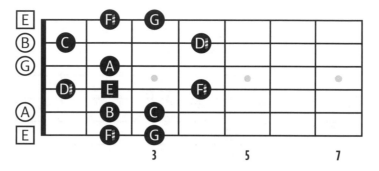

Exercise

Play the E harmonic minor scale like this, saying the note names out loud, until you have it memorized.

Tip: The note D# can also be called E♭ in other contexts.

F Major (Introducing B♭)

The F major scale is constructed from natural notes with the exception of the note B♭. The notes of F major are F, G, A, B♭, C, D, and E. There are just two B♭ notes in 1st position.

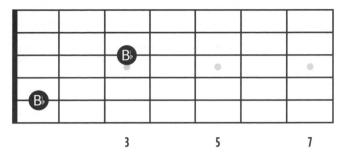

Here is the F major scale in 1st position:

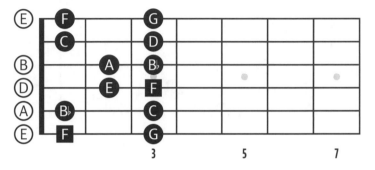

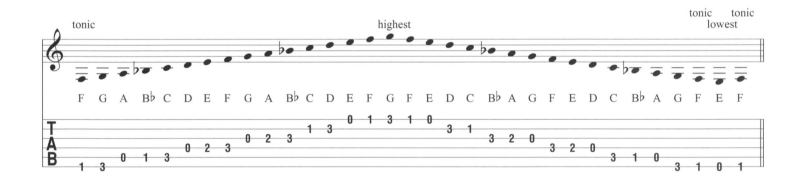

Exercise

Play the F major scale like this, saying the note names out loud, until you have it memorized.

Tip: The note B♭ can also be called A♯ in other contexts.

D Harmonic Minor (Introducing C#)

D minor is the relative minor of F major. This means that the D harmonic minor scale shares the notes of F Major, with one exception: C is raised to C#. So the notes of D harmonic minor are D, E, F, G, A, Bb, and C#. There are two occurrences of C# in 1st position.

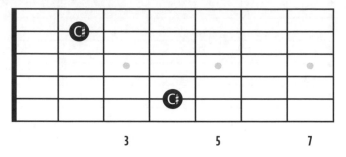

Here is the D harmonic minor scale in 1st position:

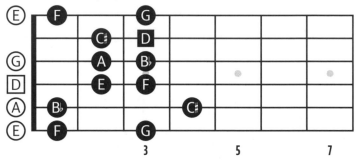

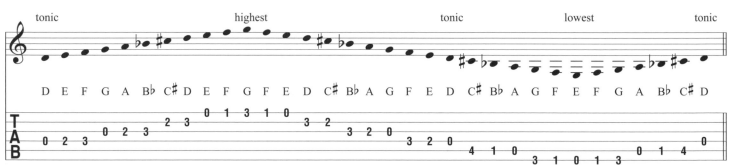

Exercise

Play the D harmonic minor as shown in the previous example, saying the note names out loud until you have it memorized.

Tip: The note C# can also be called Db in other contexts.

Recap/Notes

In this chapter, we have learned all of the notes in 1st position.

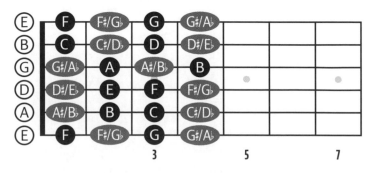

Note: Because of the way the guitar is tuned, the note B (G string, fourth fret) is the same pitch as the open B string. In any of the scales in this chapter that have an open B, a fretted B could be used instead.

CHAPTER 2: THE CHROMATIC SCALE AND DIATONIC MOVEMENT

Unlike the major and major scales, the chromatic scale uses every available note—both naturals and sharp/flats. It makes an excellent practice tool for many reasons; we can use it to revise every note in 1st position.

In order to give the sharp and flat note names equal weight in this memorization exercise, we will use the sharp names when ascending and the flat names when descending. This also makes logical sense for other reasons, and it is a pattern we'll see repeated for some other scales. We've also included the sign for the natural notes (♮) when they need to be played.

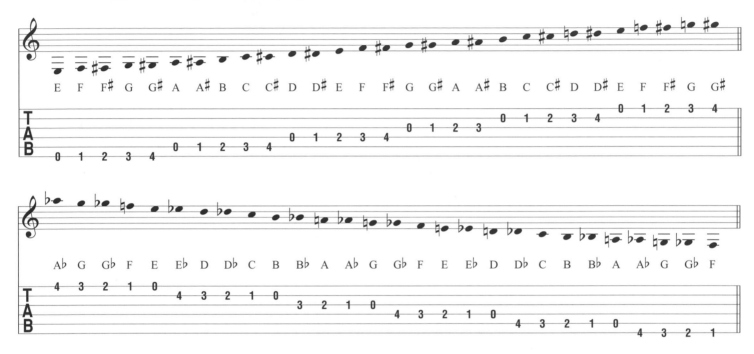

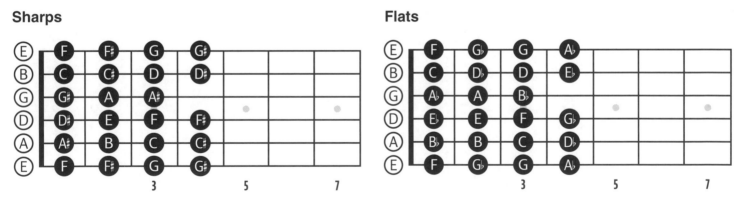

Exercise

Play the 1st position chromatic scale as shown above, saying the note names out loud until you have it memorized.

Tips:

- Remember to not play the note B (G string, fourth fret or the open B string) twice; if you do, say the name twice.

- Note that there are no sharp/flat notes between the adjacent notes B–C and E–F; on the piano, there are no black notes here either. Later, we will occasionally see note names such as B♯ and C♭, but these are physically the same notes as C and B, respectively.

The Low E String

Learning the names of notes on the low E string provides an excellent frame of reference for further exploration, which we'll continue in later chapters. Along with the A string, knowing the low E string will help you find the majority of moveable chord shapes from any root, allowing you to play almost any song in any key.

Let's begin with the E string notes at marker frets before we fill in the gaps.

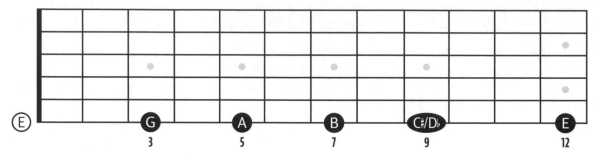

Power Chord Memorization Exercises

A simple, two-note **power chord** can be used to generate memorization exercises for these notes. The following exercises use E5, G5, A5, B5, and C#5 (Db5) power chords with the root on the low E string. The E5 shape may be played with an open E string (as shown below) or at the 12th fret as appropriate; use whichever version is closest to the other chords in the exercise. The rhythmic pattern is not important, but remember to say each chord name or root note as you play it.

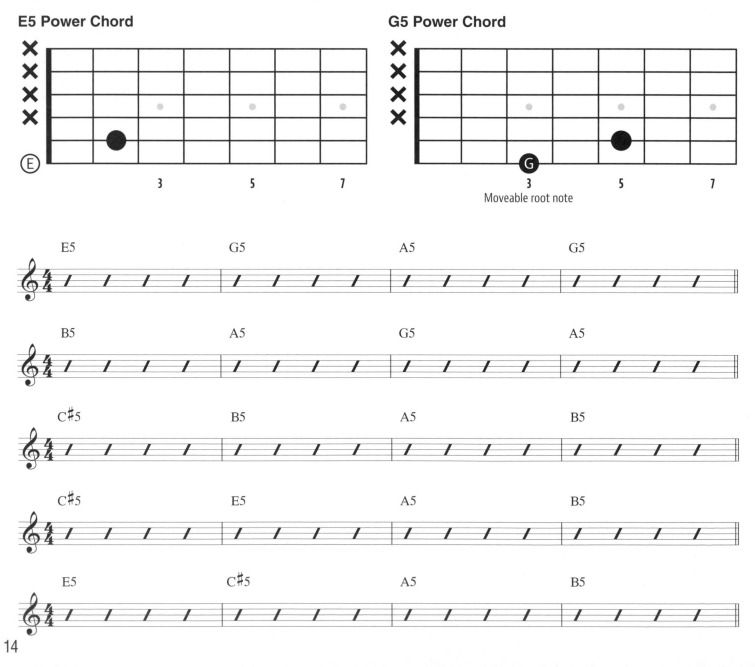

Filling the Gaps

The next step is to fill in the notes between those found at the fret markers.

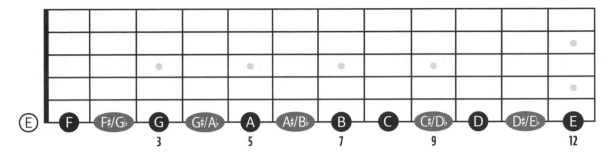

The following exercises divide the notes/chord roots above into chunks, filling in the gaps found in the previous exercises. As with the chromatic scale, we are using sharps when ascending and flats when descending.

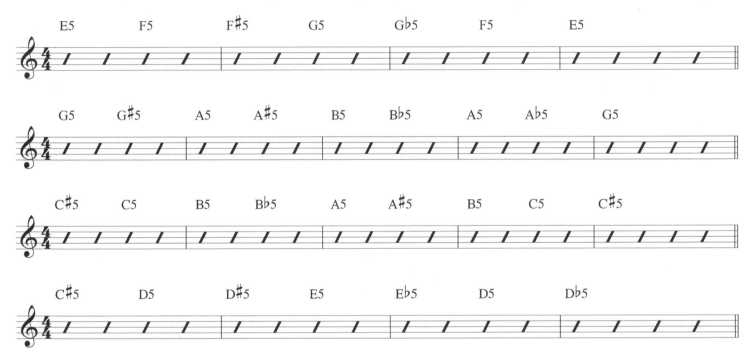

Diatonic Power Chord Exercises

The next exercises group all the low E string power chords into musical contexts using the I–vi–IV–V chord sequence. Here, we are only using the sharp/flat chord name that belongs to each key.

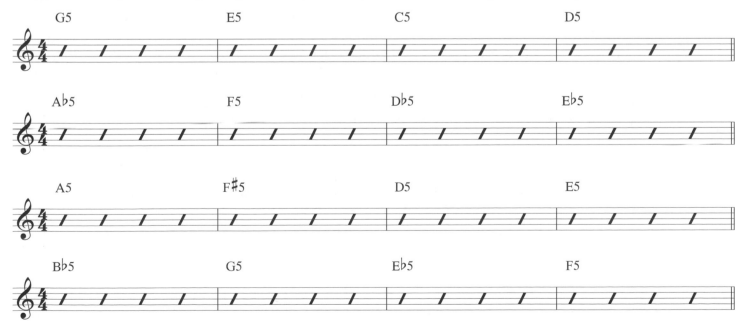

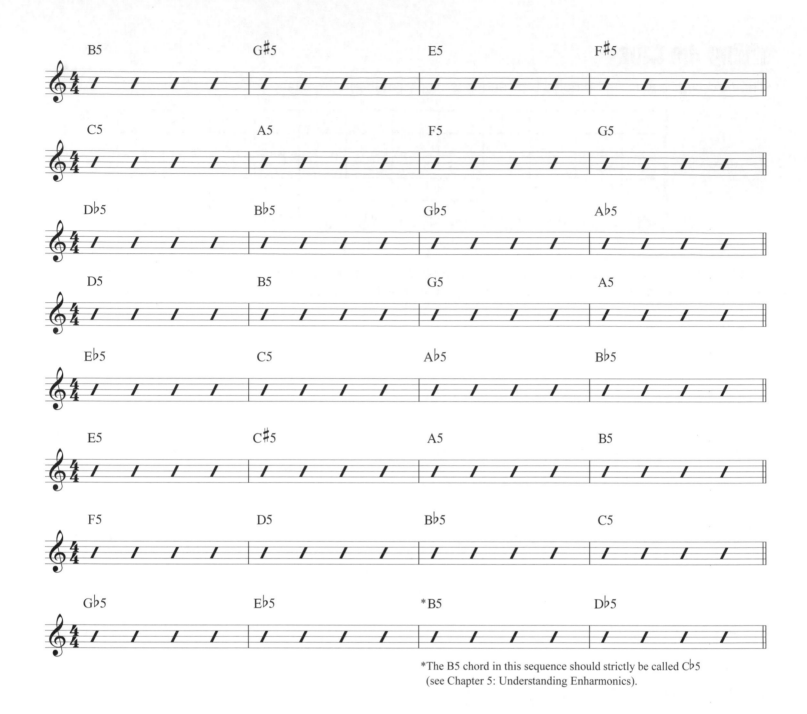

*The B5 chord in this sequence should strictly be called C♭5
(see Chapter 5: Understanding Enharmonics).

The A String

After the E string, the notes at marked frets on the A string form the next part of the puzzle that is the entire fretboard. Moveable chords with a root on the E or A string together constitute a large portion of the chord vocabulary used by pop and rock players. Here are the note names at these frets:

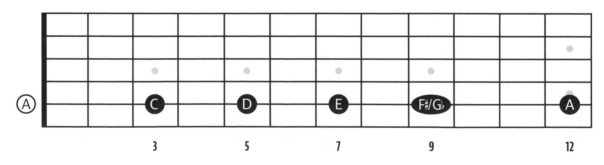

Power Chord Memorization Exercises

The following exercises use A5, C5, D5, E5, and F#5 (Gb5) power chords with the root on the A string. As with the E string exercises, the A5 shape may be played with an open A string (as shown below) or at the 12th fret as appropriate.

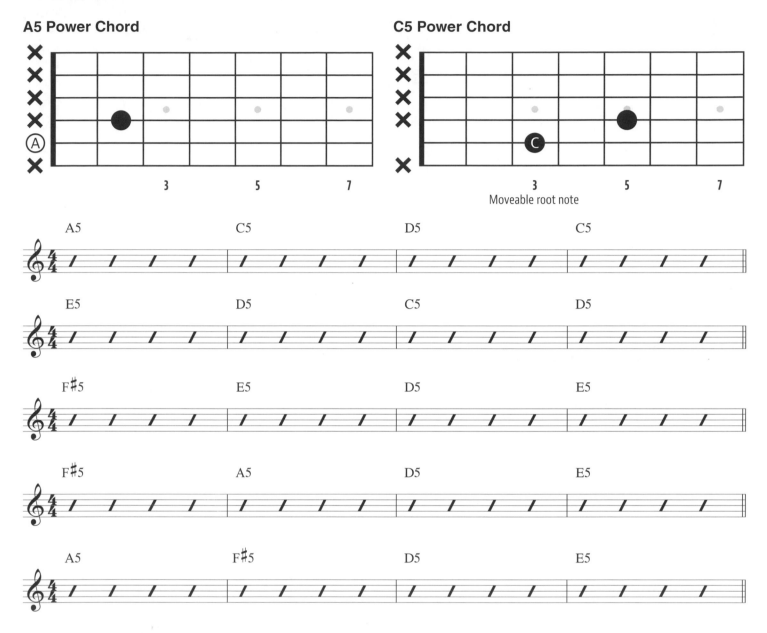

A5 Power Chord

C5 Power Chord

Moveable root note

| A5 | C5 | D5 | C5 |

| E5 | D5 | C5 | D5 |

| F#5 | E5 | D5 | E5 |

| F#5 | A5 | D5 | E5 |

| A5 | F#5 | D5 | E5 |

Filling The Gaps

The next step is to fill the notes in between the fret markers.

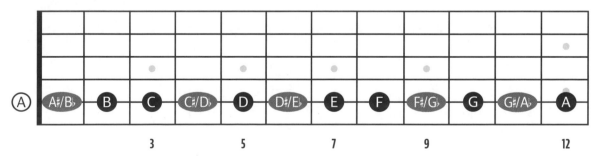

Power Chord Exercises–All Notes

Again, these exercises use both sharp and flat note names.

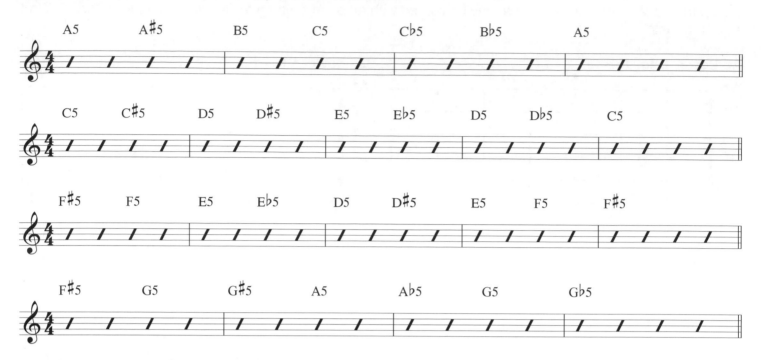

Diatonic Power Chord Exercises

Like the corresponding E string exercises, each exercise here belongs in the key of the first chord and goes around the I–iv–IV–V sequence.

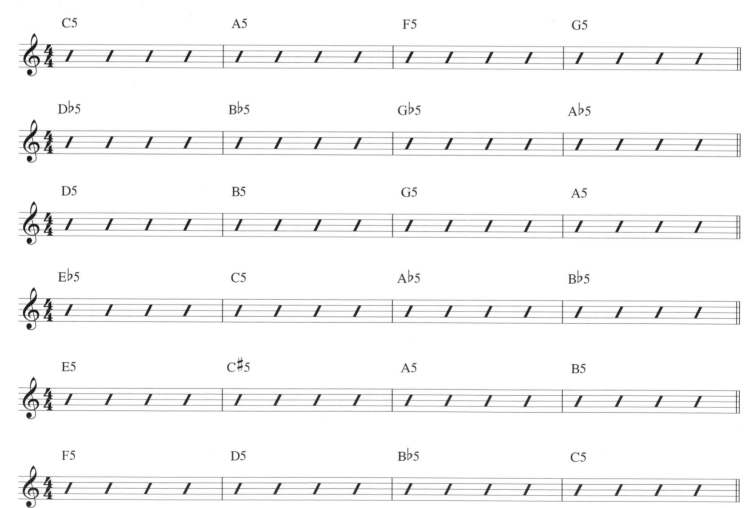

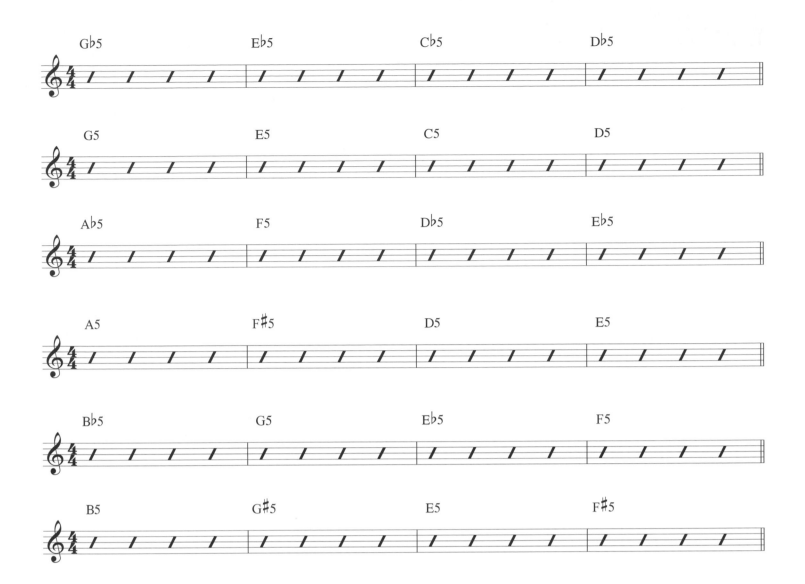

Combining the Low E String and A String Exercises

To really solidify your knowledge of the E and A strings, these exercises stay within a single, five-fret fretboard area, using either E- or A-string root chords as required. Enharmonic equivalents are mixed here to help you reach familiarity with all names.

Frets 1–5

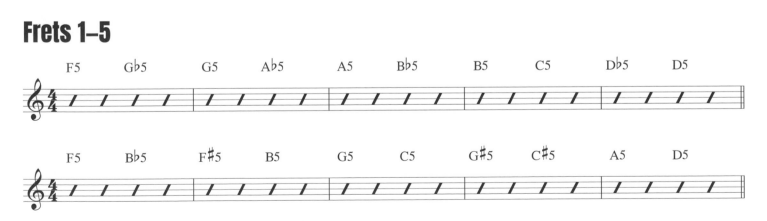

Frets 5–9

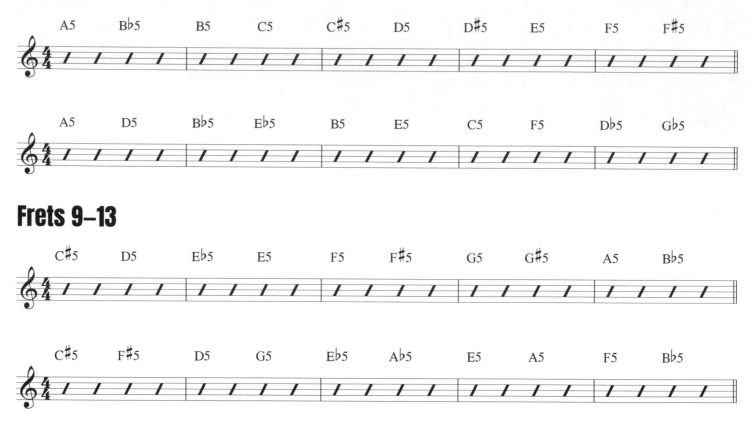

Frets 9–13

CHAPTER 3: UNDERSTANDING KEY SIGNATURES AND ENHARMONICS

Key Signatures

When we encountered sharps and flats in Chapter 1, they were simply added to individual notes as required. When they are required in order to define the **key** of a piece of music (in other words, predominant notes of a given scale), sharps or flats are instead placed at the beginning of each line to indicate that all notes of a particular letter name are to be made sharp or flat.

Examples

1. A sharp sign on the F line indicates all F♯ throughout (G major).

2. Flat signs on B and E indicate B♭ and E♭ throughout (B♭ major).

Enharmonics

Many notes are named differently depending on the context. For example, the note between F and G may be named either F♯ or G♭. In fact, all notes have alternative names. These are known as **enharmonic equivalents** or **enharmonic spellings**. It is important to become familiar with all these names and to understand the principles governing their use.

Common Sharps and Flats

Even for guitarists, it can be helpful to think in terms of visualizing notes on the piano keyboard. Here, the white notes are named using the letter names from A to G (repeating) and are known as naturals. (The black notes are the sharps and flats.) As we have seen, there are black notes between all adjacent pairs of white notes, except for E–F and B–C. The black notes are labeled below as both sharps and flats:

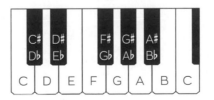

It is important to memorize these basic enharmonic equivalents:

$$C\sharp = D\flat$$
$$D\sharp = E\flat$$
$$F\sharp = G\flat$$
$$G\sharp = A\flat$$
$$A\sharp = B\flat$$

One Letter Per Step

The Western major-minor tonal system uses letters from A to G to identify all notes. All major and minor scales (and the modes derived from them) are constructed using one letter per step. This means that if one step of a scale is some kind of C (natural, flat, or sharp), then the next step has to be some kind of D (natural, flat, or sharp). The name used for any given note is always a matter of musical context, relating to the key, scale, or chord in which it is found.

For example, when constructing the G major scale, our basic major scale construction rules (see Chapter 5) dictate that the seventh note has to be the note between F and G. In another context, this could be called G♭, but here the letter G is already in use, so the note has to be called F♯.

Similarly, constructing an F major scale requires that the fourth note be some kind of B. As the note must be a half step above the third degree of the scale, it has to be a B♭; it could never be an A♯, as the letter A is already taken.

Sharp Keys and Flat Keys

As we have seen, key signatures are used to define which notes will be made sharps or flats by default in the key of a piece of music and to define how the notes in any key or scale are named. The One Letter Per Step rule also implies that conventional key signatures may contain sharps or flats, but not both. Key signatures are therefore often classified and memorized according to the number of sharps or flats they contain.

Sharp Keys

C major	No sharps or flats
G major	F♯
D major	F♯ C♯
A major	F♯ C♯ G♯
E major	F♯ C♯ G♯ D♯
B major	F♯ C♯ G♯ D♯ A♯
F♯ major	F♯ C♯ G♯ D♯ A♯ E♯
C♯ major	F♯ C♯ G♯ D♯ A♯ E♯ B♯

Flat Keys

C major	No sharps or flats
F major	B♭
B♭ major	B♭ E♭
E♭ major	B♭ E♭ A♭
A♭ major	B♭ E♭ A♭ D♭
D♭ major	B♭ E♭ A♭ D♭ G♭
G♭ major	B♭ E♭ A♭ D♭ G♭ C♭
C♭ major	B♭ E♭ A♭ D♭ G♭ C♭ F♭

The last two keys in both categories introduce notes we have not seen yet: E♯, B♯, C♭, and F♭. From a first glance at the piano keyboard on page 21, these notes simply should not exist—there are no black notes between the white notes with these letter names. Raising E by a half step takes us straight to F, so in fact, E♯ and F are physically the same note. Likewise, B♯ = C, C♭ = B, and F♭ = E.

These enharmonic spellings become necessary because of the One Letter Per Step rule. For example, for the seventh step of the F♯ major scale, the letter F is already taken. However, the note we need, though physically the same as F♮, occurs between D♯ and F♯ in the scale. Therefore, it must be given the name E♯.

The final three key signatures of each type are also interesting because they overlap; B, F♯, and C♯ are the same physical notes as C♭, G♭, and D♭, as are the scales and keys with their corresponding names. A piece written in D♭ major could equally well be written in C♯ major. In isolation, D♭ would normally be preferred in this case (seeing five flats makes for easier sight-reading than seven sharps), but there may be valid reasons for using either spelling in each case.

Double-Sharps and Double-Flats

Taking the above idea further still introduces some more obscure enharmonic equivalents. These equivalents are only rarely encountered, especially in rock and pop music, but it is nonetheless important to be aware of them. The sharp keys above are added to the table moving around what is known as a circle of fifths—each new key is a perfect 5th above the preceding key. The next sharp key after C♯ would be G♯; therefore, its seventh step has to be some kind of F.

However, the note we need is physically the same as G♮ and therefore has to be called F𝄪 (pronounced "double sharp"). This means that the note F is raised by two half steps. There is rarely any good reason to write music in the key of G♯ major rather than A♭ major (its enharmonic equivalent), nor in any other keys with double-sharps or double-flats (a given note lowered by two half steps). However, there are other uses including minor scales/keys and chromatic chords where their use is the only correct solution.

The double-sharp symbol resembles an X, while the double-flat symbol looks like two flat symbols squeezed together. Some examples are shown below:

F𝄪   C𝄪   G𝄪   B♭♭   E♭♭   A♭♭

Enharmonics and Memorization

Generally, any scale or arpeggio in this book appears in only one of its possible enharmonic guises, but it is nonetheless important to remember the other possible names. The name used here usually makes the most sense in relation to the type of scale, arpeggio, or chord; this means that some major and minor scales from the same tonic note will be viewed differently. For example, D♭ major is a "friendlier" key than C♯ major (five flats vs. seven sharps), whereas C♯ minor makes much more sense than D♭ minor.

CHAPTER 4: INTRODUCING INTERVALS

Any two notes can be described in terms of the pitch difference between them. These differences are known as **intervals** and are defined by how many note names you must count to get from one to the other, for example a 2nd, (C, D), 3rd, (C, D, E) and so on. On the guitar, intervals correspond to fixed physical relationships which can be memorized; this is enormously helpful to every aspect of guitar playing, including helping to locate any note anywhere on the fretboard by association with other known notes.

Intervals

The Octave

The **octave** is a special interval which can also be described as an eighth. As Western music uses seven note names, counting inclusively through eight notes brings us back to the starting note an octave higher: C D E F G A B C. Two notes an octave apart always share the same name and sound the same in many ways. The octave is the most consonant interval, as the two notes do not create any kind of tension or chord quality.

On the guitar fretboard, there are four basic octave shapes to be found within any single position or fretboard area: two forward-facing shapes (because the higher note is found at a higher fret) and two backward-facing shapes (because the higher note is found at a lower fret).

Forward-Facing Octaves

These octave shapes are always two strings apart, and either two or three frets apart.

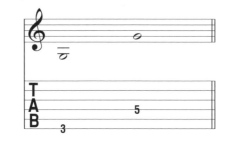

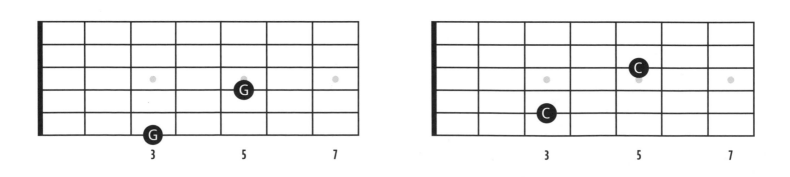

24

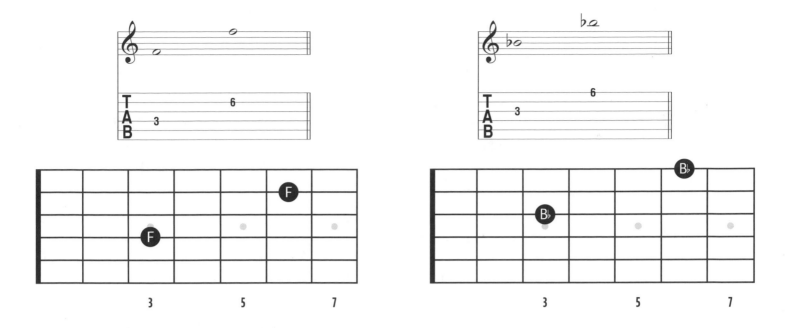

Backward-Facing Octaves

These are two strings apart, and either two or three frets apart.

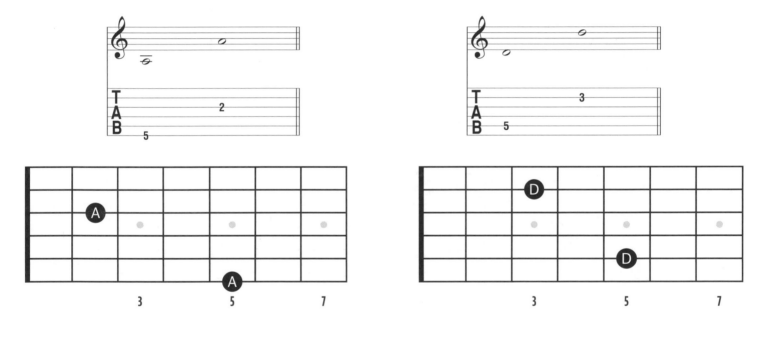

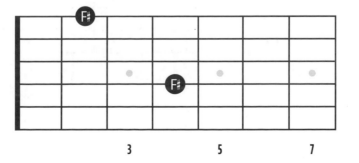

Exercises

1. Start on any known note. Using both forward- and backward-facing octave shapes, find as many other notes of the same name as you can in the first 12 frets (or beyond).

Example:

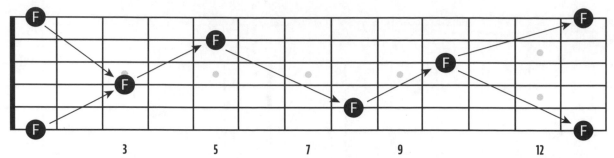

Play the resulting intervals simultaneously. You'll soon get used to the sound of the octave interval; any mistakes will jump out, as the resulting intervals will have a very different sound.

2. Work your way through the known notes on the low E string (from Chapter 2), finding (and saying aloud) the notes one and two octaves higher, using the forward-facing octave shapes.

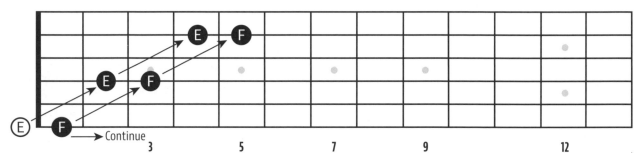

3. Repeat Exercise 2, but starting on the A string.

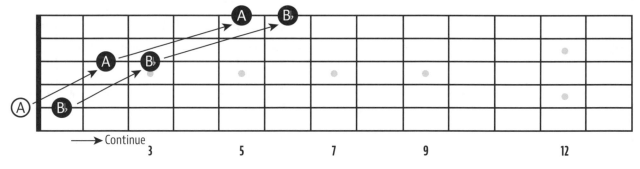

4. Work your way through the known notes on the high E string (which mirrors the low E string), from G upwards, finding the octave below each known note on the G string. From the fifth-fret A upwards, you can also add the second octave down.

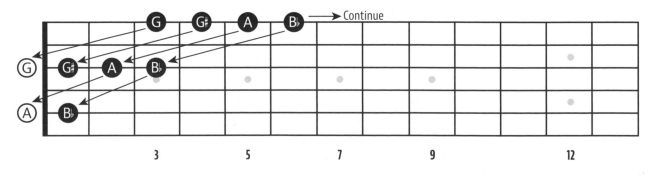

5. Work your way through the known notes on the high E string. Using backward-facing octave shapes, find the notes one and two octaves lower on the D string.

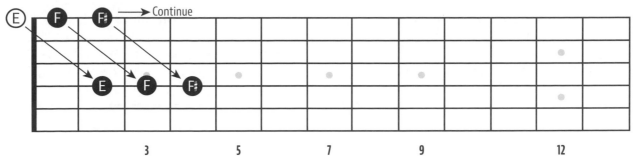

Fifths

The next interval to explore in the same way is the **5th**, or more accurately the **perfect 5th**. After the octave, this is the next most important interval to be able to find anywhere on the guitar.

Two notes a perfect 5th apart can be defined as inclusively having five note names between them. To ensure the interval is a perfect 5th, sometimes one or both of the notes will be sharp or flat. All notes separated by a single dash below are a perfect 5th apart. Use this for reference when working through the exercises that follow.

C - G - D - A - E - B - F♯ - C♯ - G♯ - D♯ - A♯
G♭ - D♭ - A♭ - E♭ - B♭ - F - C

(See also Chapter 3: Understanding Key Signatures and Enharmonics)

On the guitar, perfect 5ths are found on adjacent strings, two frets apart on all pairs, except the G and B strings, where they are three frets apart.

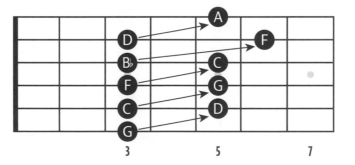

Exercises

Work your way from known notes on the low E string. From each, find and name the note a perfect 5th above, then above this, continuing until you reach the high E string or the end of the fretboard.

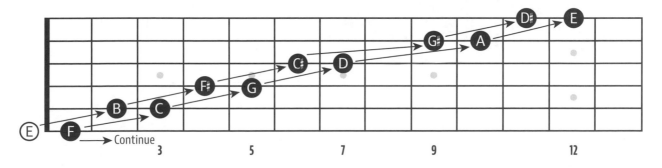

Whole Tones

The interval of a **major 2nd**, also known as a **whole tone** (also called a **whole step**), is the interval between two notes that are two frets apart on the same string. If you have internalized the note names on the E string or A string, you will already be able to recall the names of any whole tone note pairs (for example, C–D or Ab–Bb). If not, here's the low E string again for reference:

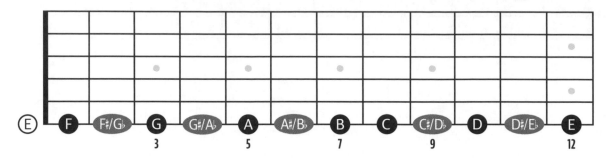

Note: As the interval name "2nd" implies, a whole tone always encompasses two adjacent letter names (for example, C–D or A–B). Depending on the context, the whole tone interval between the second and fourth frets here should therefore be written F#–G# or Gb–Ab, but never F#–Ab or Gb–G#.

Major 2nds are also found between adjacent strings, and this is where they become more useful for memorization purposes. Like the perfect 5th, the pattern is easy to remember: from the first note, go to the next string and back three frets, except between the G and B strings, where it's back two frets.

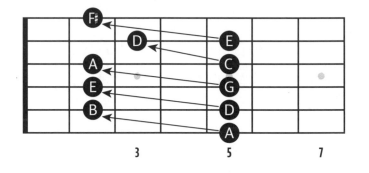

Exercises

Starting from a known note on the low E string, find the next two major 2nds. Then, skip to the A string, find the next note in the series (three frets back), and continue.

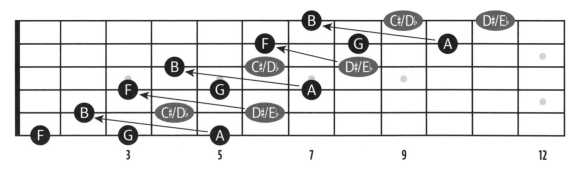

Thirds

The interval of a **3rd** (C–E, D–F, etc.) can be described as either a **major 3rd** or a **minor 3rd**, depending on how many whole tones and half tones it encompasses. The major 3rd is made up of two whole tones (for example, C to E: C–D + D–E), whereas the minor 3rd consists of a whole tone plus a half tone (D to F: D–E + E–F).

Thirds are central to the construction of chords and triads, which we'll explore later, and they are also used in their own right in many styles of music. In addition to these uses, exploring 3rds will help support your overall knowledge of the fretboard.

Major and minor 3rds are found on adjacent strings. Like 5ths and 2nds, each shape is the same between all string pairs, except for the G and B strings.

Major Third

To find a major 3rd from a given root note, go to the next string and back one fret, except between the G and B strings, where both notes are at the same fret.

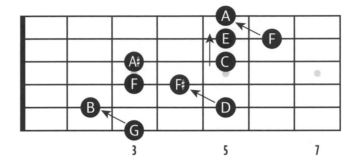

Minor Third

The upper note of a minor 3rd is one fret lower than the major 3rd. For all string pairs (except the G and B strings), the upper note is two frets back. Between the G and B strings, it's one fret back.

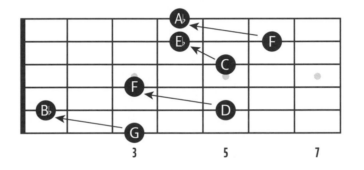

Exercises

The aim here is to gain familiarity with major and minor 3rds all over the fretboard, while also reminding yourself of the names of both notes of each interval.

1. Starting on the low E string, find and name the major 3rd (on the A string) above each known E string note. Remember that non-naturals can be described as either sharps or flats, and a 3rd interval should always encompass three letters. For example, if we are describing the low E string, second fret as F♯, then its corresponding major 3rd is A♯. Alternatively, it's G♭–B♭; the interval is never spelled F♯–B♭ or G♭–A♯.

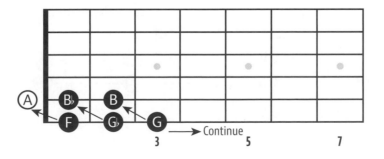

Repeat the exercise above, starting on the A, D, G, and B strings.

2.   Starting on the low E string, find and name the minor 3rd (on the A string) above each note.

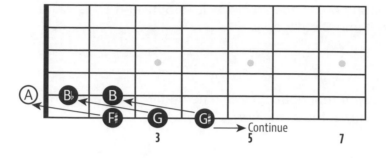

Repeat the exercise above, starting on the A, D, G, and B strings.

Diatonic Thirds

To use 3rds in a musical context, we need to combine the major and minor 3rds that belong to the key. For each 3rd, both notes need to belong to the key; this will result in both major and minor intervals. Take C major as an example:

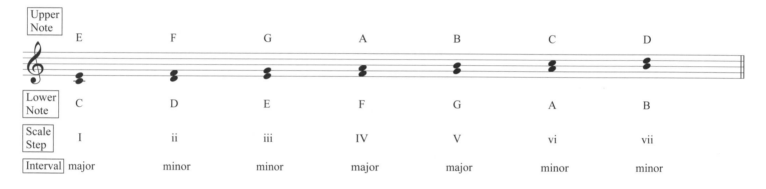

Note that major 3rds are built on the first, fourth, and fifth steps of the major scale. On the other steps, minor 3rds occur.

Exercises

1.   Find diatonic thirds in the key of F major between the low E and A strings, starting from the lowest F on the fretboard (low E string, first fret). Remember to observe the pattern above and also to refer to the scale construction of F major (see Chapter 1)—all notes should be naturals, except for B♭. To check that you are doing this correctly, refer to the following fretboard diagram and tablature.

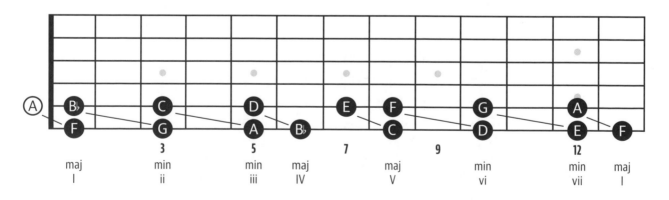

2. Repeat Exercise 1, but stay within the first five frets (including open strings), moving through adjacent string pairs as necessary. Check your findings against the tablature below.

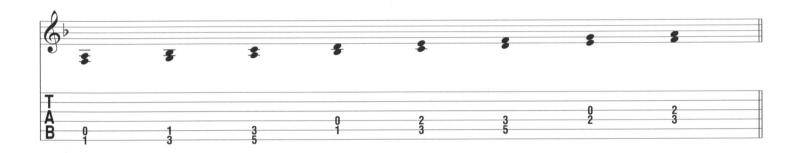

3. Continue Exercise 2 to cover the next octave; (the final F and A will take you up to the sixth fret of the B string and against the fifth fret of the high E string. Check this against the tablature below.

4. Repeat Exercises 1–3 above for the following keys, accounting for the required sharps and flats as shown in the key signatures.

G Major (F#)

Ab Major (Bb, Eb, Ab, Db)

A Major (F#, C#, G#)

CHAPTER 5: EXPLORING THE MAJOR SCALE

Major Scale Construction

The **major scale**, which we already alluded to in Chapter 1, is one of the most important building blocks in all Western music, and it's helpful to be familiar with all aspects of its construction and application on the guitar.

All major scales have the same internal construction, which is why they all sound the same regardless of key. This is a combination of whole tones (major 2nds) and half tones, also known as minor 2nds—the smallest interval between notes on most instruments. On the guitar, this is the interval between two adjacent fretted notes on any given string.

As we have seen, the C major scale is comprised of whole tones and half tones. Consecutive natural notes are mainly separated by a whole tone, except the pairs B–C and E–F, which are each separated by a half tone.

$$
\begin{array}{cccccccc}
C & D & E & F & G & A & B & C \\
(W) & (W) & (H) & (W) & (W) & (W) & (H) &
\end{array}
$$

[W = whole, H = Half]

For any major scale, the arrangement of whole and half steps is as above: whole–whole–half–whole–whole–whole–half. When building the scale from any note other than C, this means that some sharps and flats will be introduced.

Though this is not the way they are usually played on the guitar, finding major scales on a single string is an excellent way to internalize knowledge of their construction and to gain further familiarity with the notes on each string.

E Major Scale (Low E String)
Key Signature: four sharps (F#, C#, G#, D#)

Scale Notes: E–F#–G#–A–B–C#–D#–E

The note names and fret numbers are exactly the same on the high E string.

E Major Scale (High E String)
Key Signature: four sharps (F#, C#, G#, D#)

Scale Notes: E–F#–G#–A–B–C#–D#–E

A Major Scale (A String)
Key Signature: three sharps (F#, C#, G#)

Scale Notes: A–B–C#–D–E–F#–G#–A

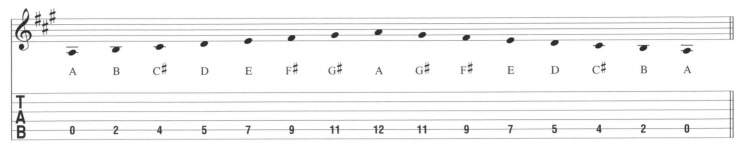

D Major Scale (D String)
Key Signature: two sharps (F#, C#)

Scale Notes: D–E–F#–G–A–B–C#–D

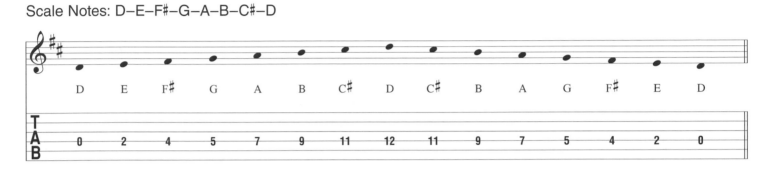

G Major Scale (G String)
Key Signature: one sharp (F#)

Scale Notes: G–A–B–C–D–E–F#–G

B Major Scale (B String)
Key Signature: five sharps (F#, C#, G#, D#, A#)

Scale Notes: B–C#–D#–E–F#–G#–A#–B

Moving all of these scales up by one half tone (starting on the first fret) not only completes the picture with the addition of the other six major scales, it also helps reinforce our knowledge of all the other fretted notes on each string up to the 13th fret.

F Major Scale (Low E String)
Key Signature: one flat (B♭)

Scale Notes: F–G–A–B♭–C–D–E–F

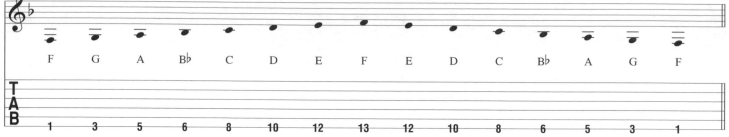

F Major Scale (High E String)
Key Signature: one flat (B♭)

Scale Notes: F–G–A–B♭–C–D–E–F

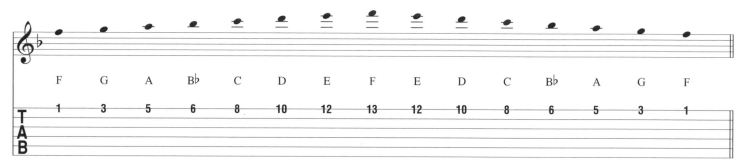

B♭ Major Scale (A String)
Key Signature: two flats (B♭, E♭)

Scale Notes: B♭–C–D–E♭–F–G–A–B♭

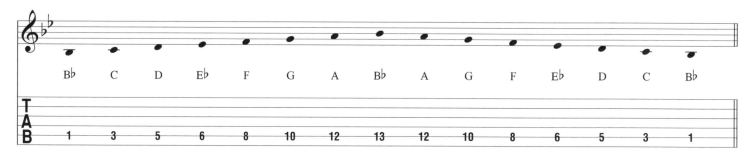

E♭ Major Scale (D String)
Key Signature: three flats (B♭, E♭, A♭)

Scale Notes: E♭–F–G–A♭–B♭–C–D–E♭

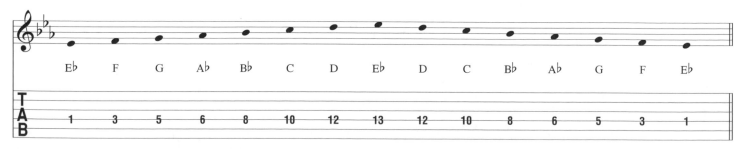

Ab Major Scale (G String)
Key Signature: four flats (Bb, Eb, Ab, Db)

Scale Notes: Ab–Bb–C–Db–Eb–F–G–Ab

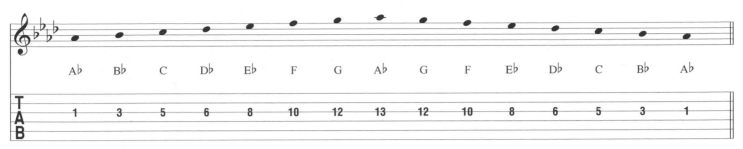

C Major Scale (B String)
Key Signature: no sharps or flats

Scale Notes: C–D–E–F–G–A–B–C

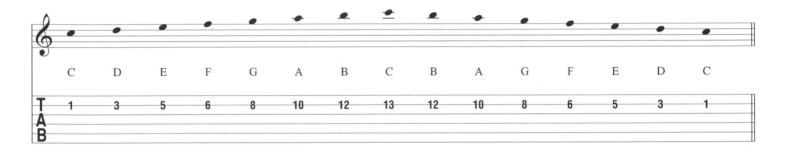

Exercises

1. Play all of the above scales, saying each note name as you go.

2. Once the scale notes of all of the above scales are familiar, try finding more single-string scales, starting from frets 2 and 3.

Vertical Major Scale Shapes (Frets 1-5)

This focuses on finding all 12 major scale in the first five frets. As with the pentatonic scale (Chapter 6), this is ultimately a prelude to being able to find all major scales anywhere on the fretboard, which becomes easier because all the shapes repeat. For now, the task at hand is to get familiar with all the shapes in the first five frets. It's pretty intense; take your time and dip into this chapter at intervals rather than trying to digest it all at once. For maximum benefit, play each scale as outlined in Chapter 1:

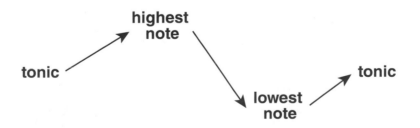

Note on Positions and Stretches

As we have four fretting fingers, a position on the guitar is usually defined as a four-fret area, with the number reflecting the lowest fret in that position. So 1st position is frets 1–4, 2nd position is frets 2–5, and so on. While some scale shapes fit neatly within a four-fret position, others require either the first or fourth finger to stretch to an adjacent fret. The technically correct way (for the moment) to approach the scales in this chapter is to observe the position given (in this case, either 1st or 2nd position), keeping all fingers at their designated frets unless performing a stretch.

1st position

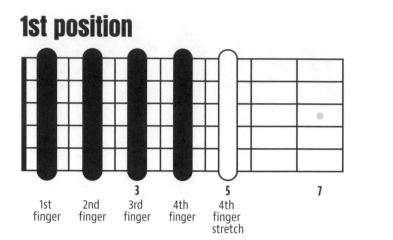

1st finger	2nd finger	3rd finger	4th finger	4th finger stretch
		3		5

2nd position

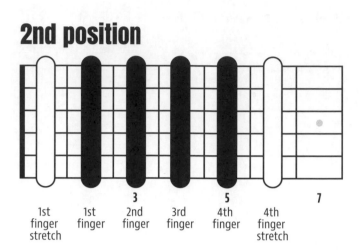

1st finger stretch	1st finger	2nd finger	3rd finger	4th finger	4th finger stretch
		3		5	

The 2nd-position, fourth-finger stretch will not be used in this chapter, as we are keeping to the first five frets. Some shapes, including the A major, B major, and E major shapes below, slightly break this rule.

F Major

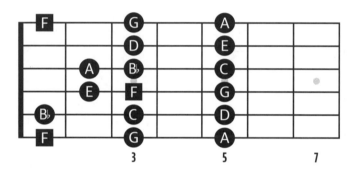

G♭ Major

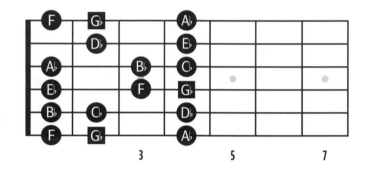

G Major

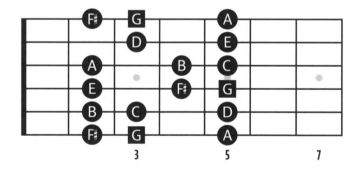

A♭ Major

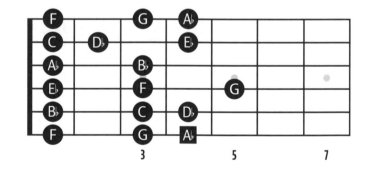

A Major

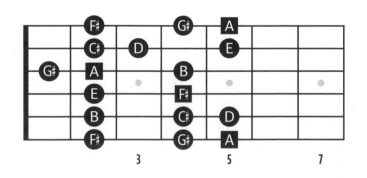

B♭ Major

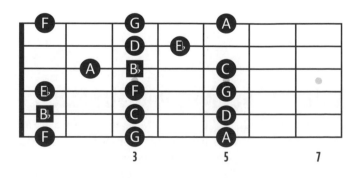

B Major

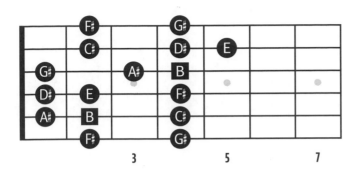

C Major

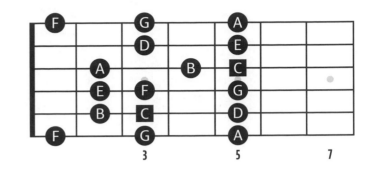

D♭ Major

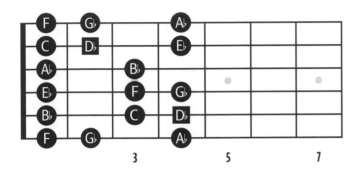

D Major

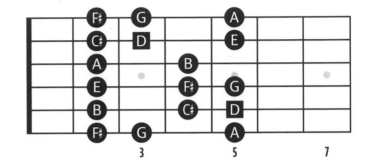

E♭ Major

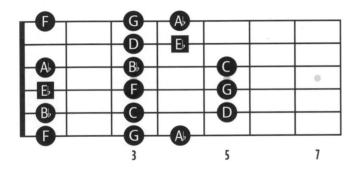

E Major

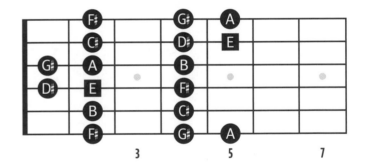

Special Fingerings

A Major: All notes are played in 2nd position except for the G string (shift back to 1st position)

B Major: All notes are played in 1st position except for the B and high E strings (shift to 2nd position)

E Major: Play all the notes located on the D and G strings in 1st position; shift to 2nd position for other strings

Exercises

The focus here is no longer about learning the locations of individual notes on the fretboard (although this is still important) so much as internalizing the scale shapes above, along with their application in this fret area. If the goal is to instinctively and instantly know where to find the notes of any scale or key in any fretboard area (and ultimately, all over the neck), it is not enough to merely play up and down each scale a few times and move on. Rather, we need to really explore them. The following exercises should first be played in F major as written, before moving on and applying the same approaches to all of the other major scales shown previously.

Ascending and Descending

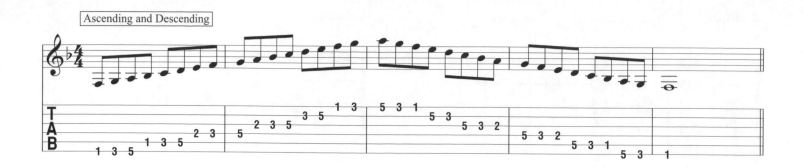

Pattern 1

Pattern 2

Pattern 3

Pattern 4

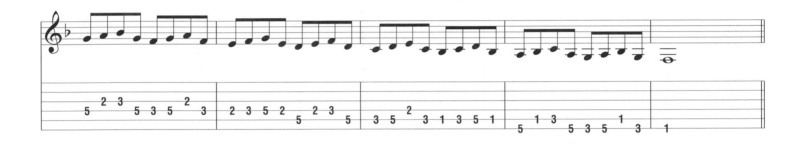

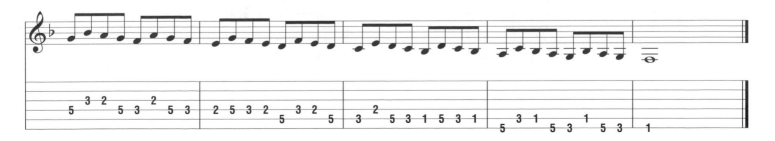

CHAPTER 6: PENTATONIC SCALES

The Pentatonic Scale

The **pentatonic scale** is simpler than the major scale; it has fewer notes and is central to the improvising approach of many players in a wide range of styles.

Just as each major scale has a relative minor, each major pentatonic scale has a relative minor pentatonic scale, which is actually the exact same set of notes, with a different note designated as the tonic. For example, F minor pentatonic and A♭ major pentatonic share the same notes. For practice purposes, play it by starting and ending on F for the F minor pentatonic scale and starting and ending on A♭ for the A♭ major pentatonic. (The minor root is indicated with a filled square while the major root is indicated with an open square.)

F Minor/A♭ Major Pentatonic

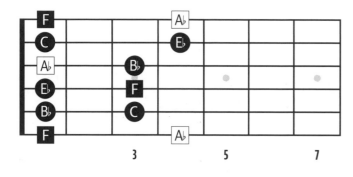

F# Minor/A Major Pentatonic

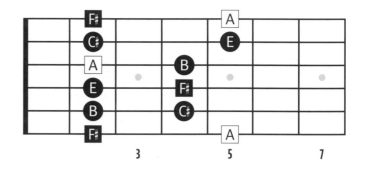

G Minor/B♭ Major Pentatonic

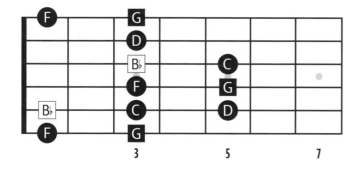

G# Minor/B Major Pentatonic

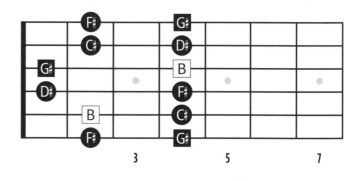

A Minor/C Major Pentatonic

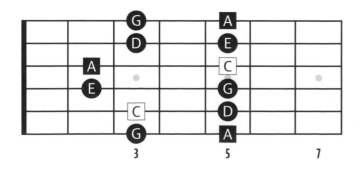

B♭ Minor/D♭ Major Pentatonic

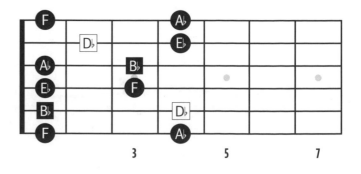

B Minor/D Major Pentatonic

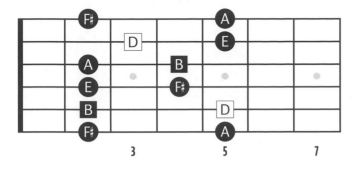

C Minor/E♭ Major Pentatonic

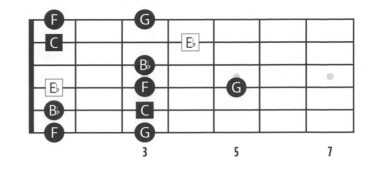

C♯ Minor/E Major Pentatonic

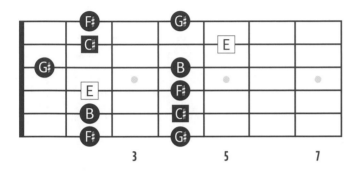

D Minor/F Major Pentatonic

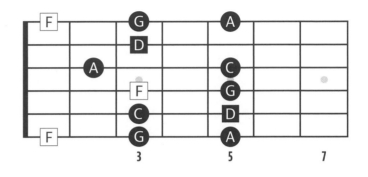

E♭ Minor/G♭ Major Pentatonic

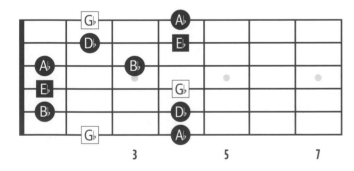

E Minor/G Major Pentatonic

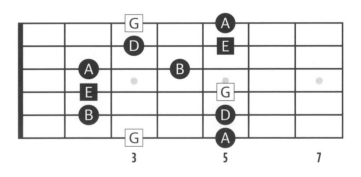

Exercises

1. Practice each of these scales, from both the major and minor tonic notes, making sure you say (or think) the name of each note as you play. Also, try to internalize the feeling of playing these shapes without looking at the fretboard; this will make it much easier to join them all together to play any given pentatonic scale all over the neck.

2. The following sample exercise should first be played as written, in F minor pentatonic. Once this is fluid, the same patterns should be applied to the rest of the pentatonic scales above.

Ascending and Descending

Pattern 1

Pattern 2

Pattern 3

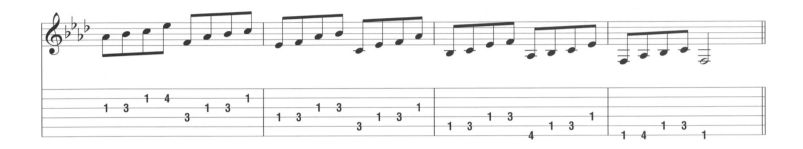

CHAPTER 7: MELODIC AND HARMONIC MINOR SCALES

Each major scale or key has a related minor scale or key, as seen briefly in Chapters 1 and 5, and again with major and minor pentatonic scales. Each major scale can also be modified to create a minor scale from the same tonic note. In fact, there are several types of minor scales that can be created in this way. This parallel approach to creating minor scales is the focus of this section.

The Melodic Minor Scale

If the third step of the major scale is lowered by a half tone, then the result is a type of minor scale called the **melodic minor scale**. For example, the third step of the C major scale (E) can be changed to E♭, resulting in the C melodic minor scale.

All of the major scale shapes from Chapter 5 can be modified to produce melodic minor scale shapes. Usually, the third step moves one fret down the string; however, the modification is sometimes a little more complicated. Here's the C melodic minor scale shown as a modified C major scale (grey) notes:

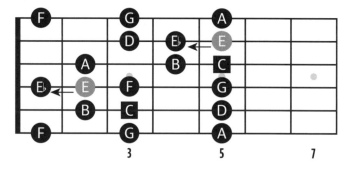

Melodic Minor Scales: Frets 1–5

F Melodic Minor

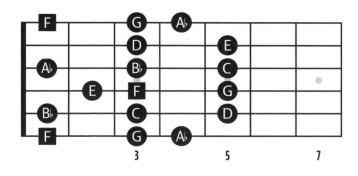

F♯ Melodic Minor

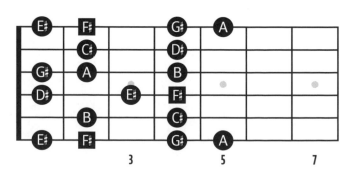

G Melodic Minor

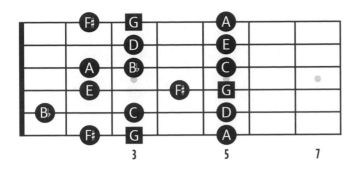

A♭ Melodic Minor

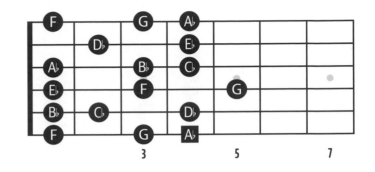

A Melodic Minor

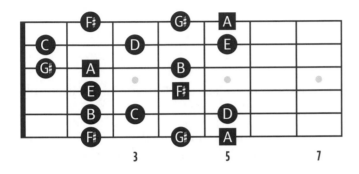

B♭ Melodic Minor

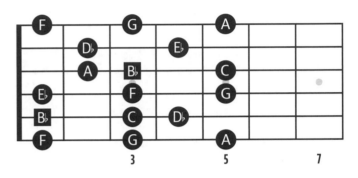

B Melodic Minor

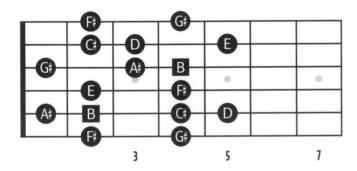

C Melodic Minor

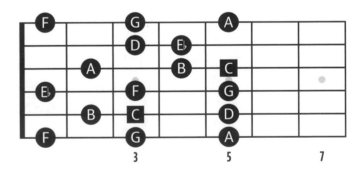

D♭ Melodic Minor

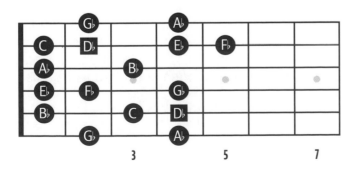

D Melodic Minor

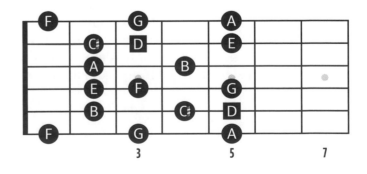

E♭ Melodic Minor   **E Melodic Minor**

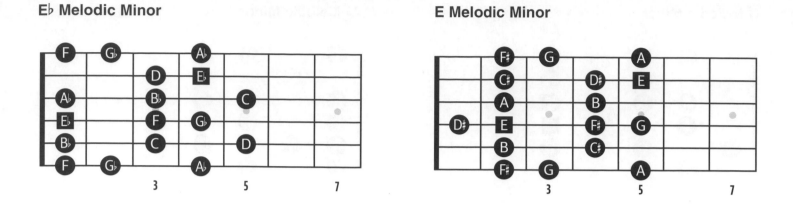

Exercises

Apply the patterns from Chapter 5 to all of these melodic minor shapes.

The Harmonic Minor Scale

Although we've already discussed the **harmonic minor scale**, in this section, we'll dive more in-depth to this scale and how it relates to the previous scales covered.

The flatted third step of the melodic minor scale is in fact common to all minor scales. To derive the harmonic minor scale from this, another step is lowered: the sixth. Returning to our example in C, the sixth step (A) is lowered to A♭.

Here is the C harmonic minor scale presented as a modified C major scale:

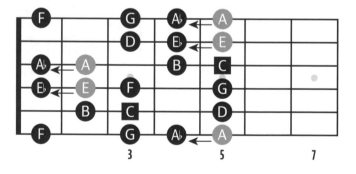

The harmonic minor scale has an unusual interval between the sixth and seventh steps (between A♭ and B in C harmonic minor): an **augmented 2nd**. This is unlike all the intervals of the major scale or melodic minor scale, which are either whole or half tones. This scale consists of three half tones, or a whole tone plus a half tone. This interval gives the harmonic minor scale its characteristic sound, which is often described as Spanish or even Arabic.

Harmonic Minor Scales: Frets 1–5

F Harmonic Minor

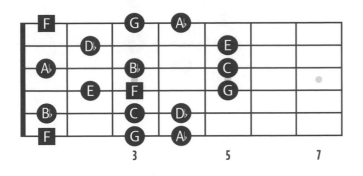

F# Harmonic Minor

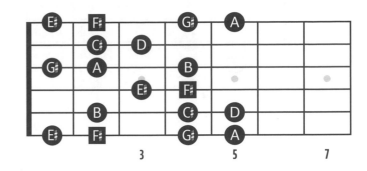

G Harmonic Minor

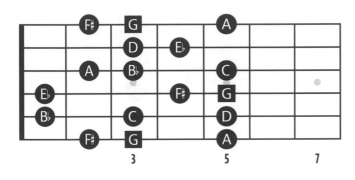

Ab Harmonic Minor

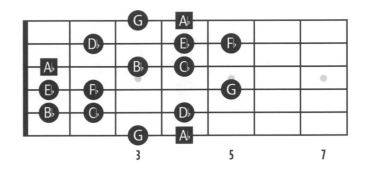

A Harmonic Minor

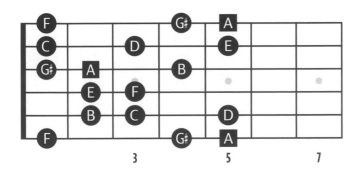

Bb Harmonic Minor

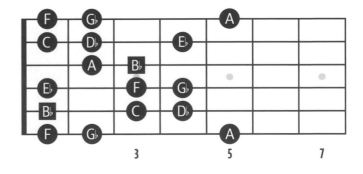

B Harmonic Minor

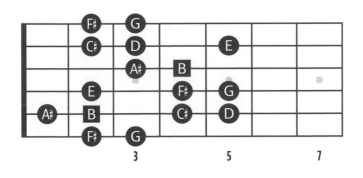

C Harmonic Minor

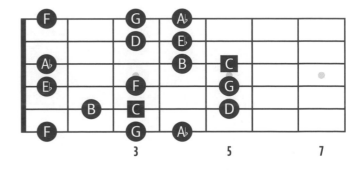

C# Harmonic Minor

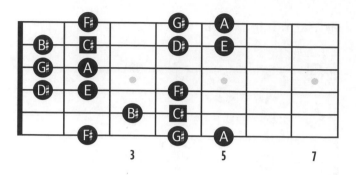

D Harmonic Minor

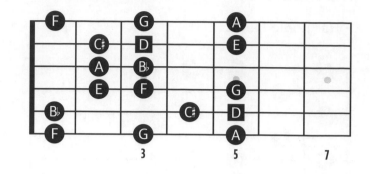

Eb Harmonic Minor

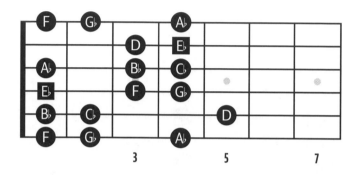

E Harmonic Minor

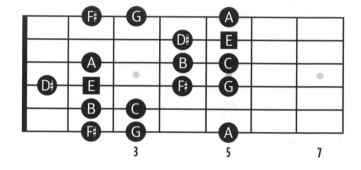

Exercises

Apply the patterns from Chapter 5 to all of these harmonic minor shapes.

CHAPTER 8: THE BLUES SCALE

The **blues scale** is essentially a minor pentatonic scale with one extra note per octave. This extra note is located between the perfect 4th and perfect 5th from the tonic note, so it can be written as either a raised 4th or flatted 5th. In the case of the C blues scale, it can either be written as F♯ or G♭. As with the chromatic scale, this is often written as a raised note in the ascending form and then as a flatted note in the descending form.

tonic   raised 4th/
flatted 5th   raised 4th/
flatted 5th   tonic

Blues Scales: Frets 1–5

F Blues

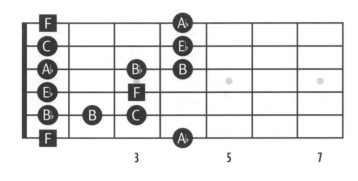

F♯ Blues

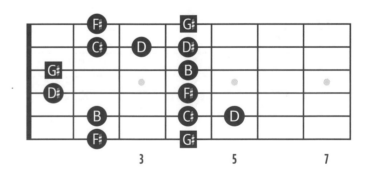

G Blues

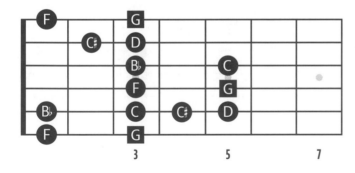

G♯ Blues

A Blues

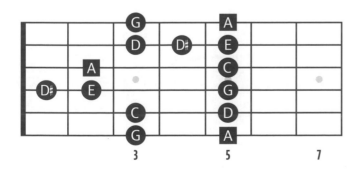

B♭ Blues

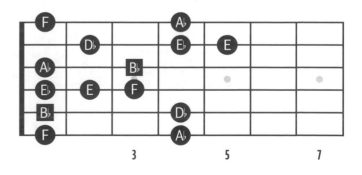

49

B Blues

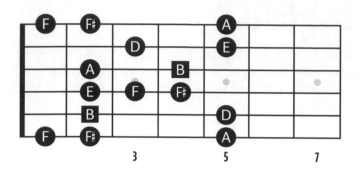

C Blues

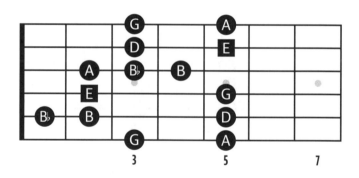

C♯ Blues

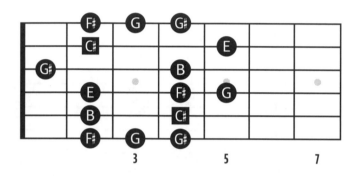

D Blues

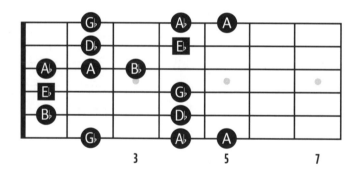

E♭ Blues

E Blues

Exercises

The sample exercise here applies the pattern-based approach to the F blues scale. This should then be transposed to all of the scale shapes shown previously.

Pattern 1

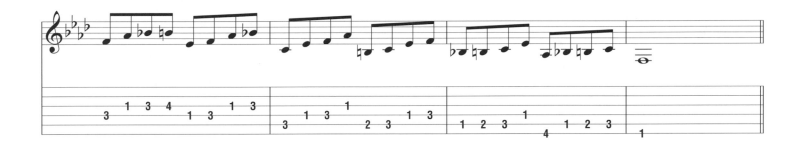

Pattern 2

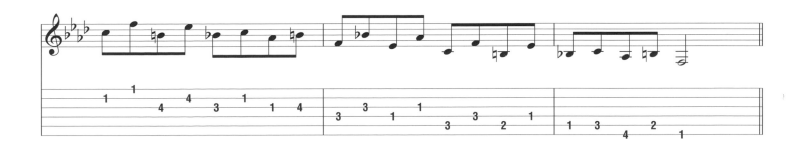

CHAPTER 9: FIRST-POSITION CHORDS

Learning a small number of easy chords in 1st position can go a long way, both in terms of reinforcing the locations of many notes in 1st position and later on by forming the basis of moveable chord shapes, which can be played anywhere on the fretboard.

E

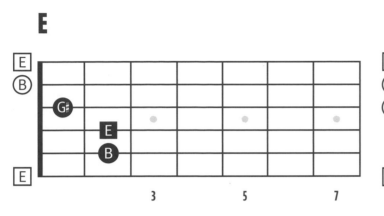

Em

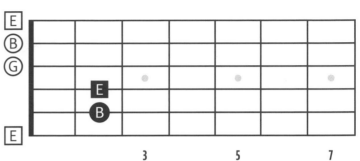

A

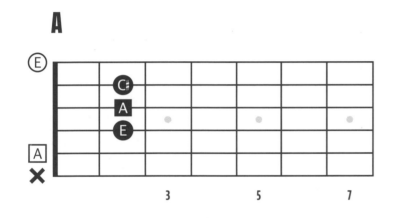

Am

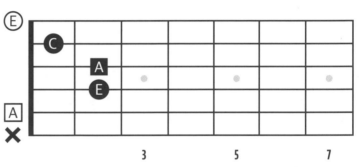

D

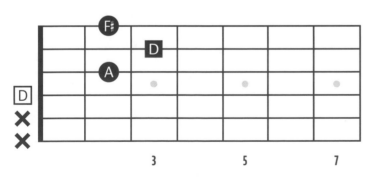

Dm

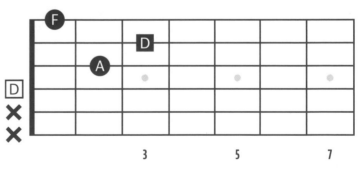

G

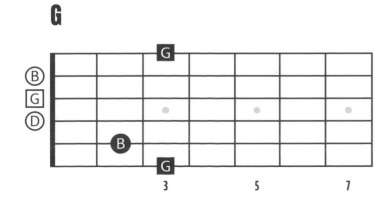

C

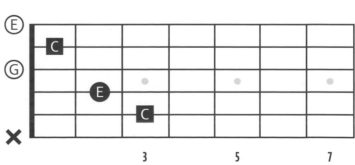

Exercises

Seventh Chords

All of these chords are derived from the major and minor chords above, and they will also form the basis of moveable shapes that can be played anywhere on the fretboard.

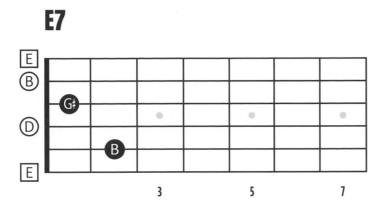

E7

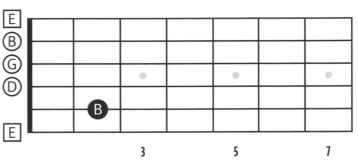

Em7

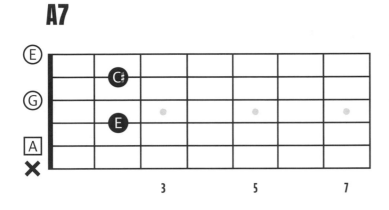

A7

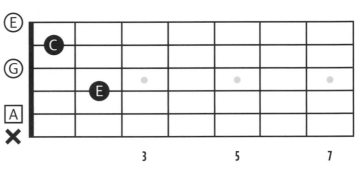

Am7

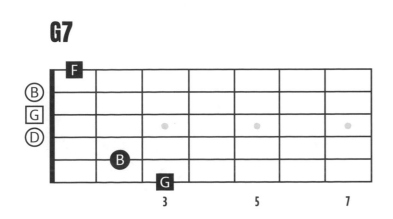

D7

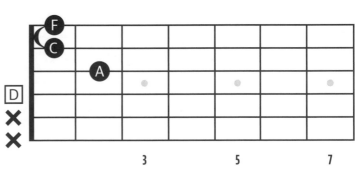

Dm7

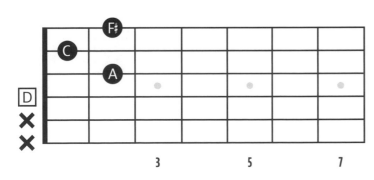

G7

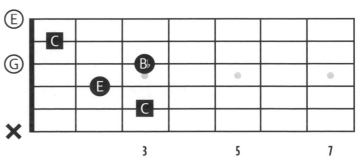

C7

Exercises

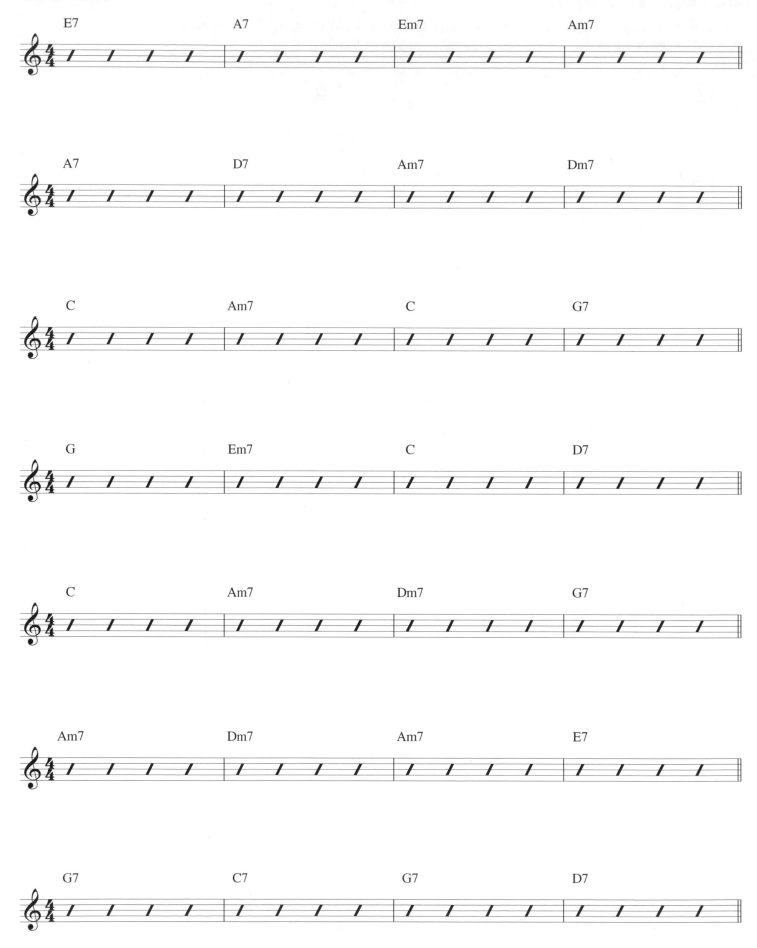

CHAPTER 10: TRIADS

When three different notes are heard together, the result is called a **triad**. Triads form the basis of Western chordal harmony. All triads are constructed by adding two notes above a root note, each a 3rd apart. As there are two types of 3rds (major and minor), there are four types of triads:

Major 3rd + Minor 3rd: Major Triad

Minor 3rd + Major 3rd: Minor Triad

Major 3rd + Major 3rd: Augmented Triad

Minor 3rd + Minor 3rd: Diminished Triad

Triad Shapes (E-String Root)

Major

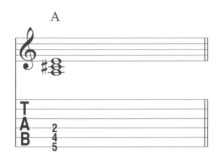

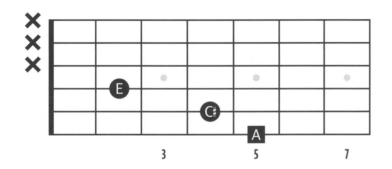

Minor

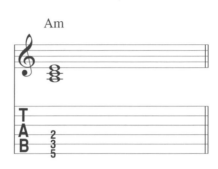

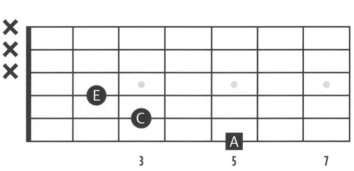

Diminished

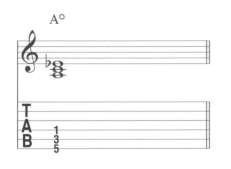

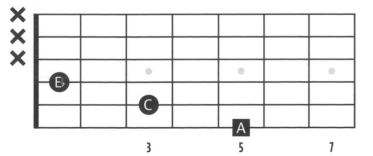

Augmented

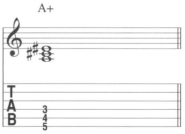

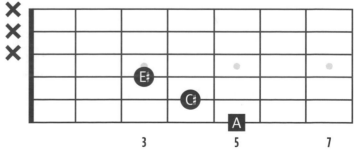

Note: The E♯ seen in the previous example is the same sounding note as F♮, but for correct musical grammar, it is named E♯. (This is because C♯–E♯ is a 3rd, whereas C♯–F would technically be a variety of 4th.)

Harmonizing the Major Scale with Triads

Just as the major scale can be harmonized in thirds (see Chapter 3), it can also be harmonized in triads. To do this, we construct a diatonic triad (one whose notes all belong in the key) from each step of the scale. The harmonization pattern is based on the pattern for thirds, with one refinement—the seventh step of the scale is harmonized with a diminished triad.

I	ii	iii	IV	V	vi	vii°
maj	min	min	maj	maj	min	dim

Let's explore how to construct an A major scale harmonized in triads. First, we need to locate the notes of the A major scale on the low E string.

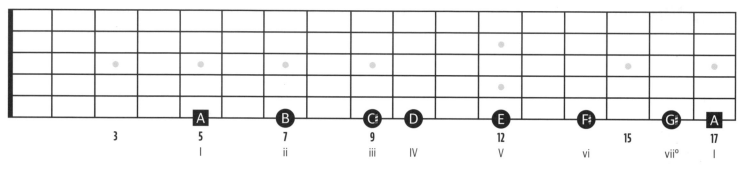

Next, we can construct the applicable triad from each scale step.

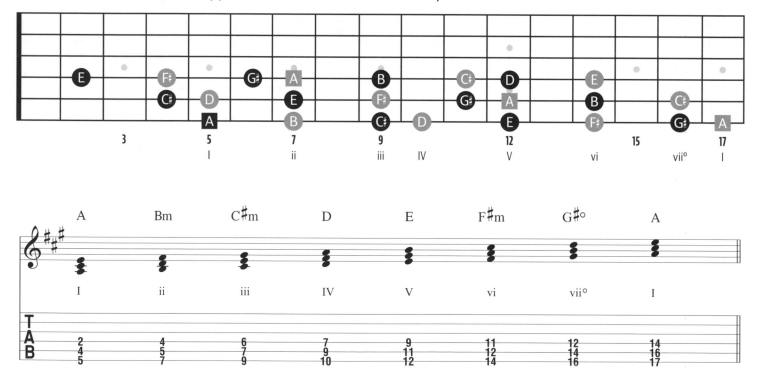

Exercise

Drawing on your knowledge of the notes found on the E string and major scale construction (Chapter 5), find the harmonized triads of the following major scales/keys: F major, G major, C major, and D major (you can harmonize more major scales if you want).

Tip: For most of these keys, you will need to start from the first note on the string from which a triad can be constructed, which will not be the tonic. For example: F is found at the first fret, so there is not enough space on the lower, adjacent frets to construct a triad. Instead, start on Gm (the second step), reaching the chord further up the string.

Triad Shapes (A-String Root)

These shapes are the same as the low E-string shapes, but they're built from the A string.

Major

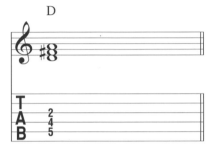

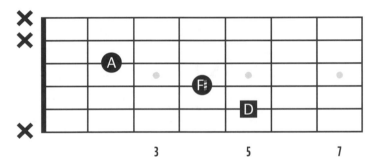

Minor

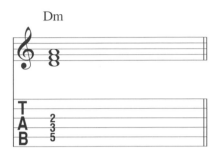

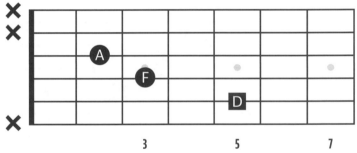

Diminished

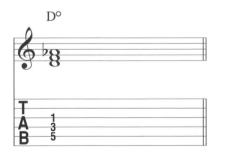

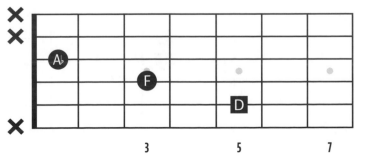

Augmented

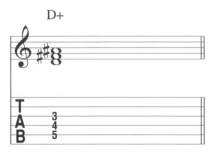

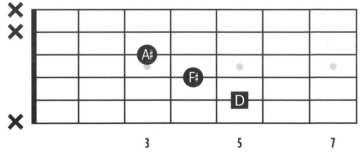

Exercises

1. Harmonize the D major scale in triads, following the A major (low E string) harmonization pattern you encountered earlier.

2. Harmonize at least the following major scales/keys on the A string: C major, D major, F major, and E♭ major. As before, many of these will require starting on a step other than the tonic.

Triad Shapes (D-String Root)

In terms of practical application, these shapes may be considered more important on the guitar, as they form the essential notes of some frequently used shapes. They also generally sound clearer than the lower-voiced shapes and are mainly easier to play. Therefore, they are worth exploring in greater detail than the lower shapes.

Major

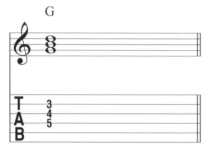

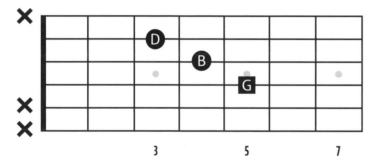

Minor

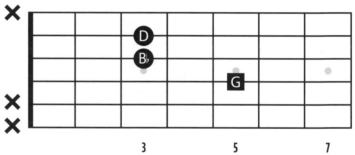

Diminished

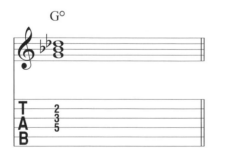

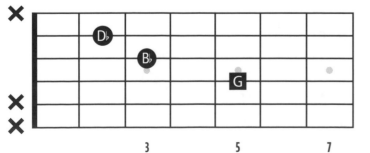

Augmented

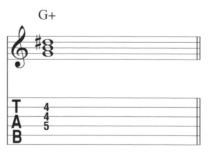

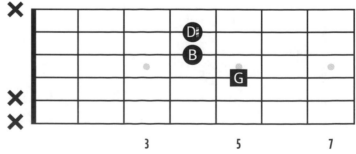

Exercises

1. To find the root note of any triad on the D string, use the octave shape from any note on the low E string.

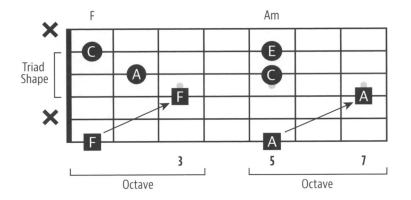

From each available root note on the D string (referring to the E string as above if necessary) find the major, minor, diminished, and augmented triad.

2. Starting on F major, harmonize the major scale in triads (major–minor–minor–major–major–minor–diminished). Continue up the fretboard harmonizing each major scale (G♭, G, A♭, etc). In the higher keys here, depending on your guitar, you will reach the point where the exercise needs to be completed by skipping down to the lower frets.

Triad Shapes (G-String Root)

Like the D-string root shapes, these shapes are important in many playing styles.

Major

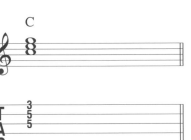

Minor

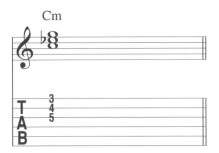

Diminished

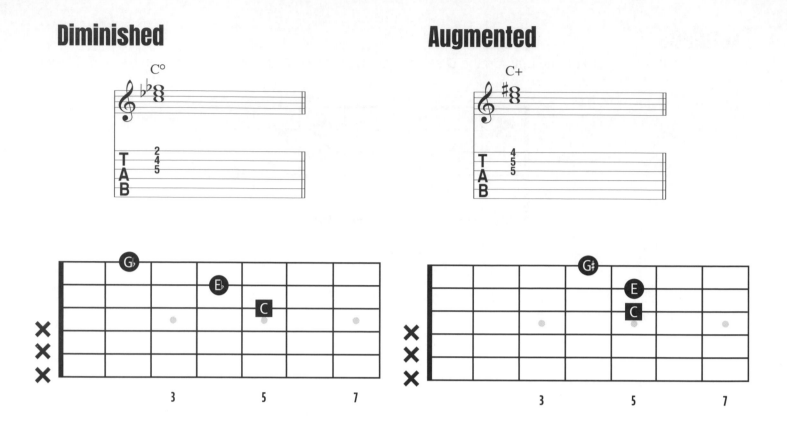

Augmented

Exercises

Repeat Exercises 1 and 2 from the D-string root shapes for G-string root shapes. If your G-string knowledge is less secure than the lower strings, remember to use the octave interval to relate back to known notes on the A string:

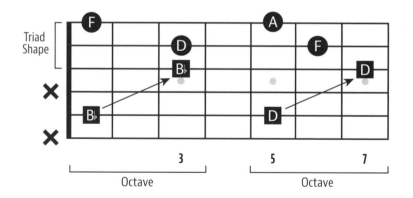

Triad Inversions

Triads are usually constructed by adding 3rds to a given root note. The outer interval between all the triads we have seen so far is a 5th:

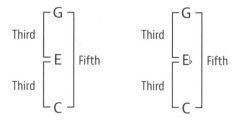

For this reason, the notes of a triad are called the root, 3rd, and 5th. However, they don't always have to be constructed in this order. A triad with the root note at the bottom is called a **root-position** triad; if the 3rd or 5th is the lowest note, this is called an **inversion** (1st and 2nd inversion, respectively). Here is a C major chord in root position, 1st inversion, and 2nd inversion:

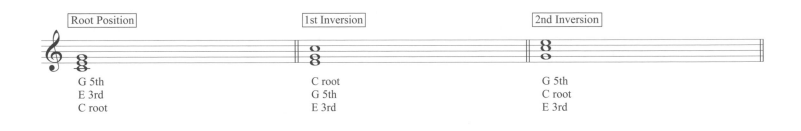

First Inversion Shapes: Low E, A, and D Strings (D-String Root)

The shapes have their root on the D string, so thinking about the name of this note within each shape is helpful both in terms of reinforcing your knowledge of the D string and also to help you easily reach for these shapes.

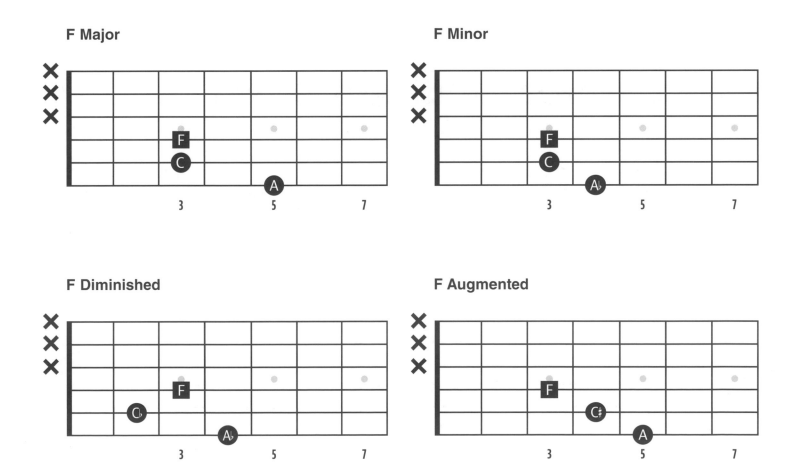

First Inversion Shapes: A, D, and G Strings (G-String Root)

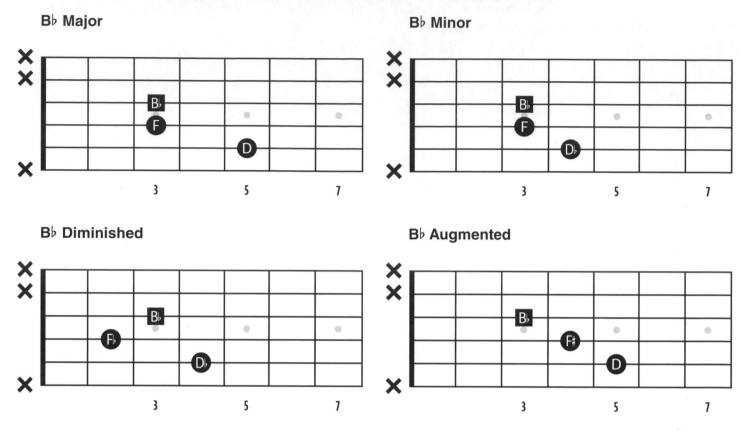

B♭ Major

B♭ Minor

B♭ Diminished

B♭ Augmented

First Inversion Shapes: D, G, and B Strings (B-String Root)

D Major

D Minor

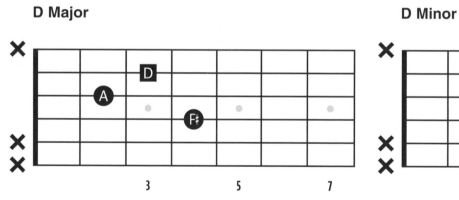

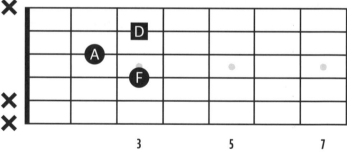

D Diminished

D Augmented

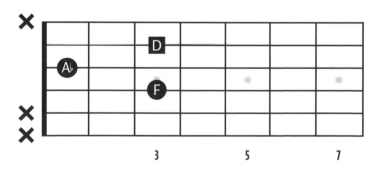

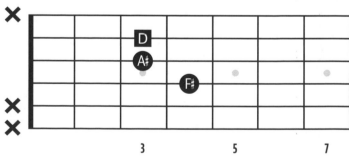

First Inversion Shapes: G, B, and High E Strings (High E-String Root)

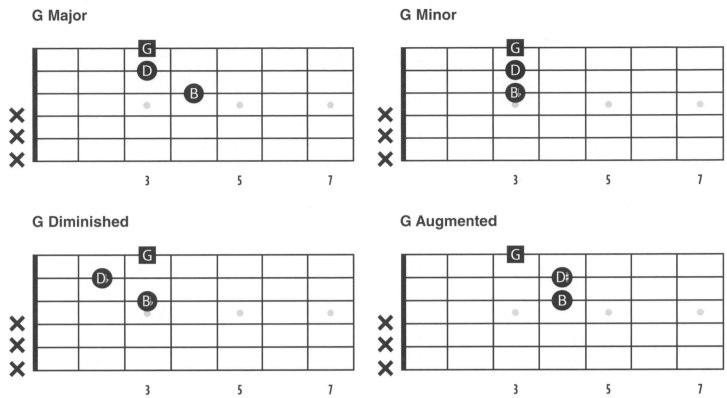

G Major

G Minor

G Diminished

G Augmented

Exercise

Starting with the lowest available major triad, harmonize the major scale (major–minor–minor–major–major–minor–diminished) using all these triad shapes. Then, repeat this exercise for all major keys. In the higher keys, depending on your guitar, you will reach the point where the exercise needs to be completed by skipping down to the lower frets.

Second Inversion Shapes: E, A, and D Strings (A-String Root)

Second inversions have the 5th on the lowest string and the root note on the middle string of the shape (in this case, the A string), so this is the note to focus on.

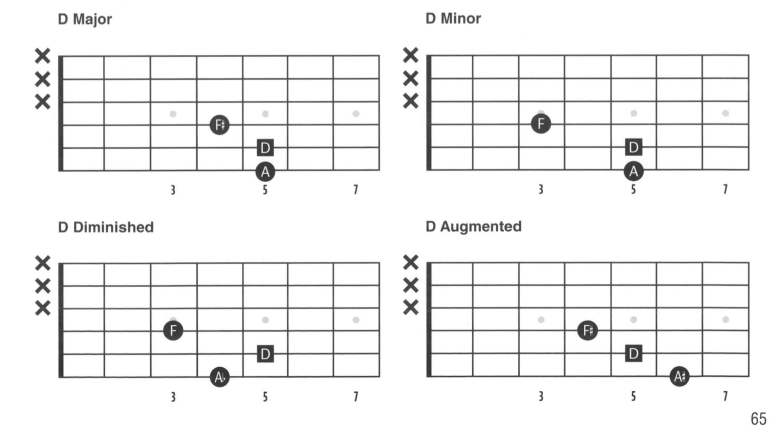

D Major

D Minor

D Diminished

D Augmented

Second Inversion Shapes: A, D, and G Strings (D-String Root)

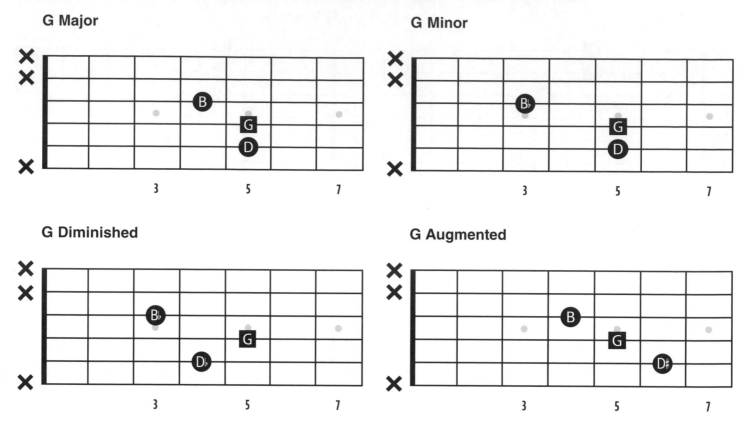

G Major

G Minor

G Diminished

G Augmented

Second Inversion Shapes: D, G, and B Strings (G-String Root)

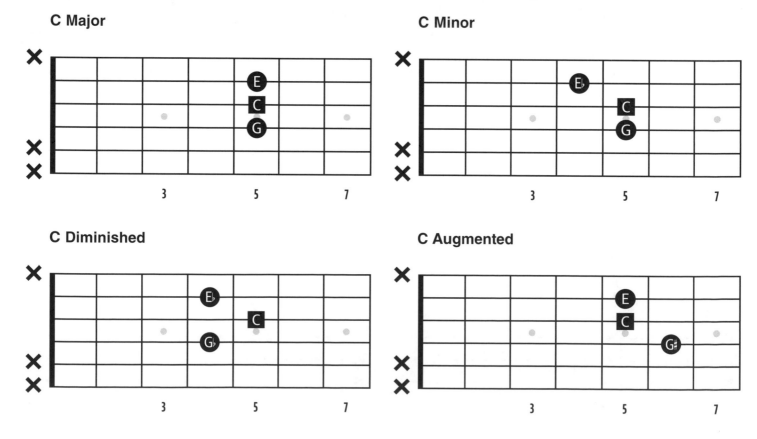

C Major

C Minor

C Diminished

C Augmented

Second Inversion Shapes: G, B, and High E Strings (B-String Root)

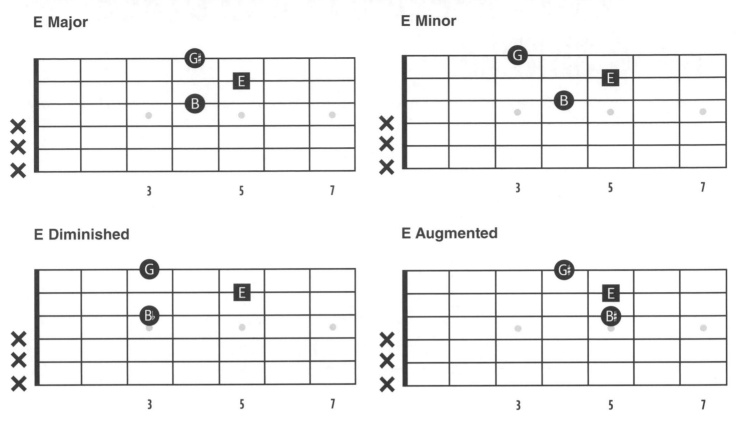

E Major

E Minor

E Diminished

E Augmented

Exercise

Harmonize each major scale using the second inversion triad shapes above.

CHAPTER 11: ARPEGGIOS AND OTHER CHORD SHAPES

When all the notes of a chord are played in sequence, this is called an **arpeggio**. Usually (and especially for practice purposes), this involves the notes of the chord in more than one octave, first ascending and then descending. On the guitar, the most useful practice pattern is the same that is used for scales: Move from lowest root note to the highest available note in that particular position, and then descend to lowest note, coming back up to root note (if applicable).

For example, the notes of the D major chord are D, F#, and A. First, let's find all of these notes within the first five frets.

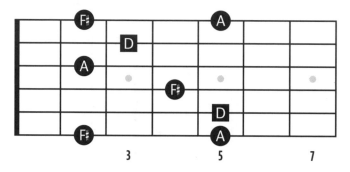

Now, let's play these notes in the sequence, from the root to the highest note, moving to the lowest note, and then back to the root.

Major Arpeggios: Frets 1–5

F Major

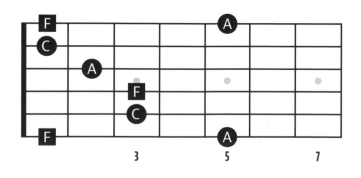

G♭ Major

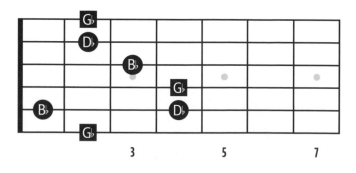

G Major

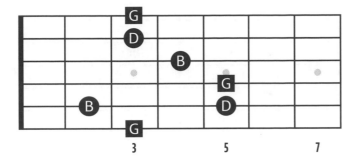

Ab Major

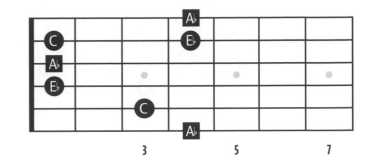

A Major

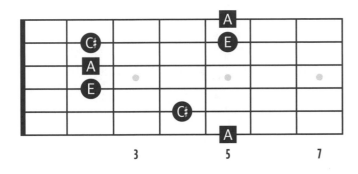

Bb Major

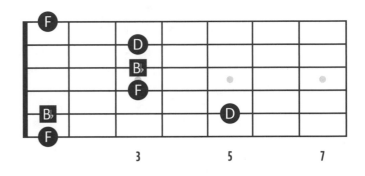

B Major

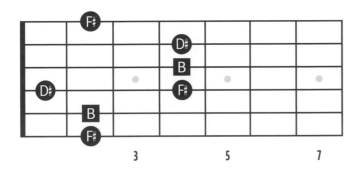

C Major

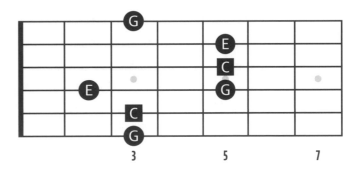

Db Major

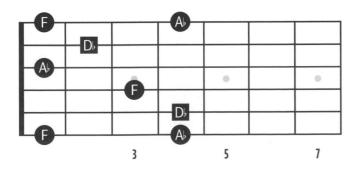

D Major

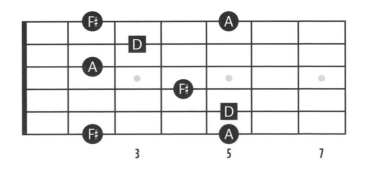

Eb Major

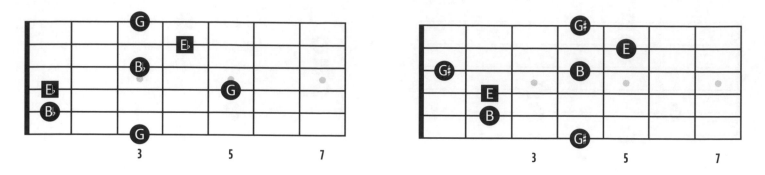

E Major

Arpeggios and Triads

If you have studied and memorized the root position, 1st inversion, and 2nd inversion triads, then you will notice that these familiar triad shapes are incorporated where the arpeggio notes fall across three adjacent strings (one note per string).

D Major (root position)

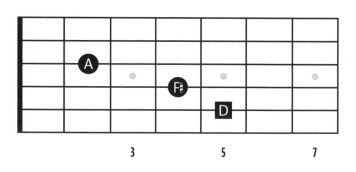

D Major (1st inversion)

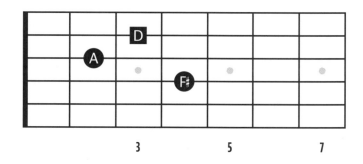

D Major (root position)

D Major (2nd inversion)

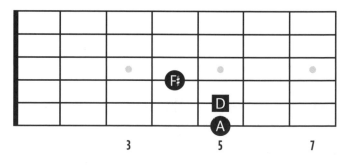

Minor Arpeggios

Just as minor scales all have a flatted 3rd compared to the major scale, we can create a minor arpeggio by flatting the 3rd of a major arpeggio. For example, the notes of the C major triad, C–E–G, become C–Eb–G.

Minor Arpeggios: Frets 1–5

F Minor

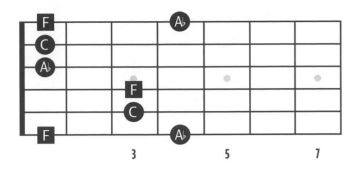

F# Minor

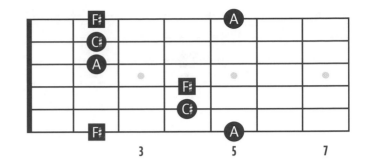

G Minor

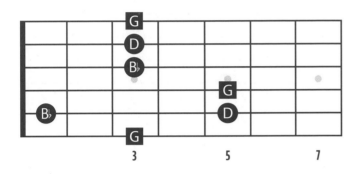

A♭ Minor

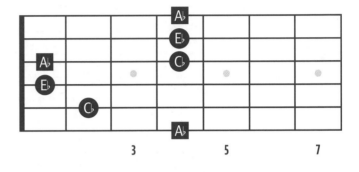

A Minor

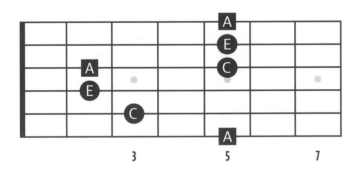

B♭ Minor

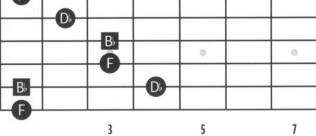

B Minor

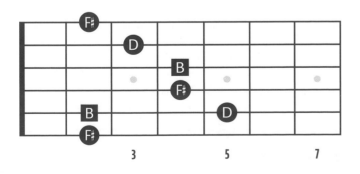

C Minor

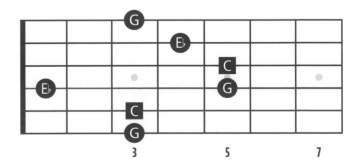

D♭ Minor

D Minor

E♭ Minor

E Minor

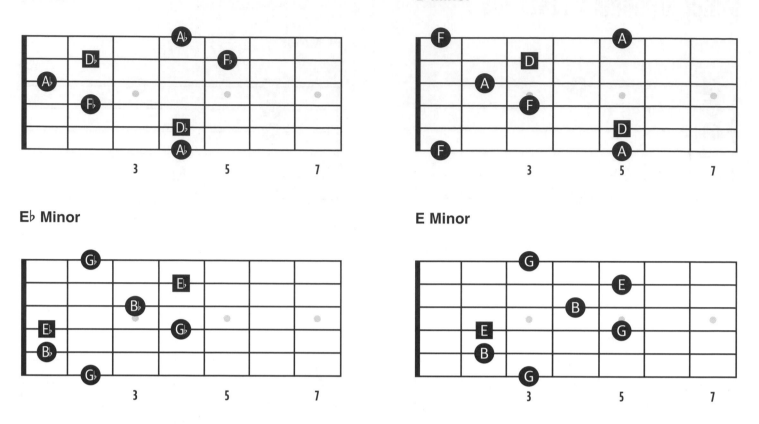

Moveable Chords

A handful of basic, moveable chord shapes can be transferred anywhere on the fretboard. This way, you can easily find the chords to almost any song you might encounter. Along the way, you can reinforce your knowledge of the low E and A strings, as all of these shapes are built from a root on one of these strings.

All of these chords are **barre chords**, meaning that they each require one finger (usually the first) to cover more than one string. All of the shapes are based on 1st-position chords found in Chapter 9, and they are shown here transposed up by one fret.

F Barre Chord (E-String Root)

B♭ Barre Chord (A-String Root)

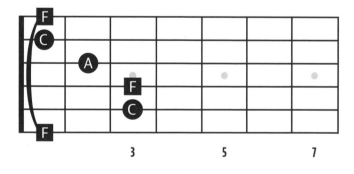

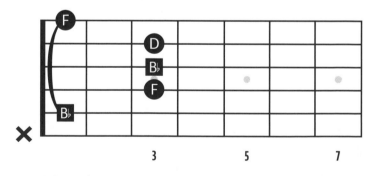

Fm Barre Chord (E-String Root)

B♭m Barre Chord (A-String Root)

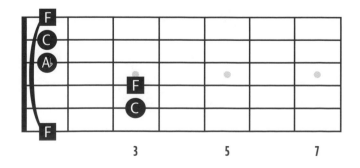

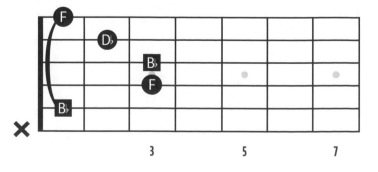

F7 Barre Chord (E-String Root)

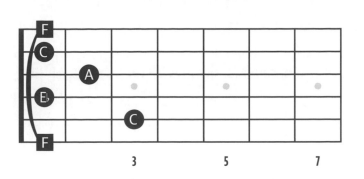

Bb7 Barre Chord (A-String Root)

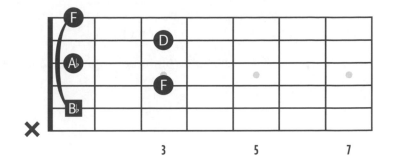

Fm7 Barre Chord (E-String Root)

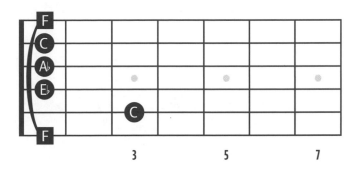

Bbm7 Barre Chord (A-String Root)

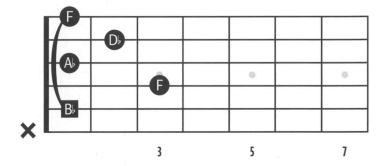

Db Barre Chord (A-String Root)

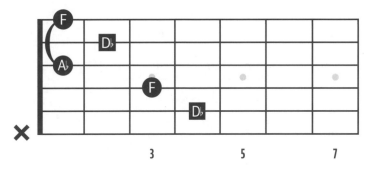

Staying within the first five frets for now, let's recap the notes on the low E and A strings, which we can use to build moveable chords:

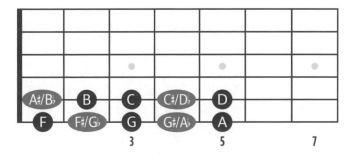

73

Exercises

The following exercises use these moveable shapes in various combinations. If in doubt, use the root finder above to locate the root note of any chord.

Note: D and D♭/C# major chords may be played using either of two shapes (shown as B♭ on page 72 and D♭ on page 73).

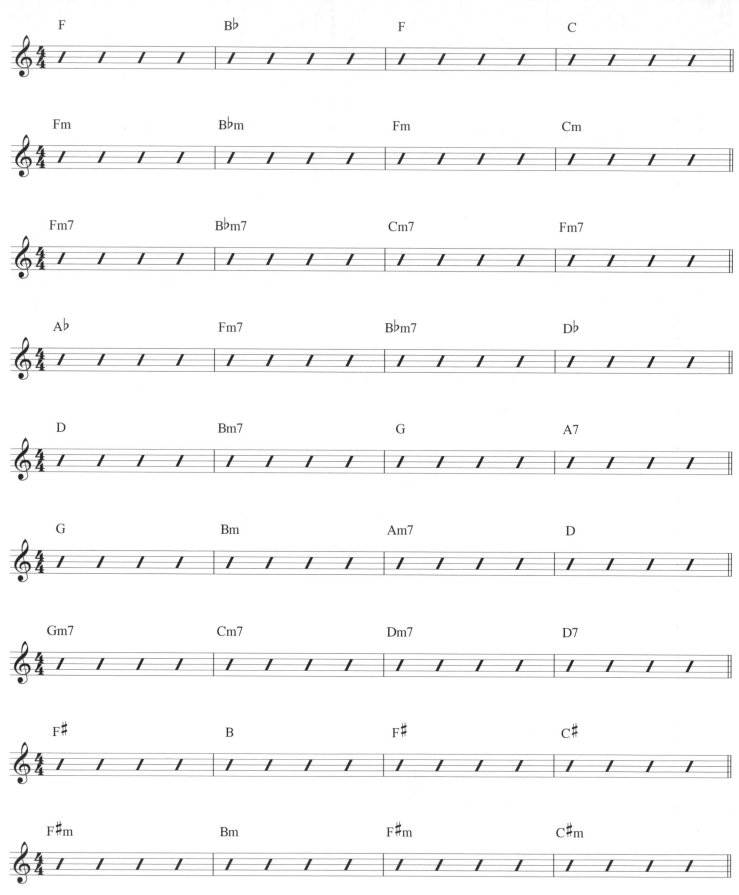

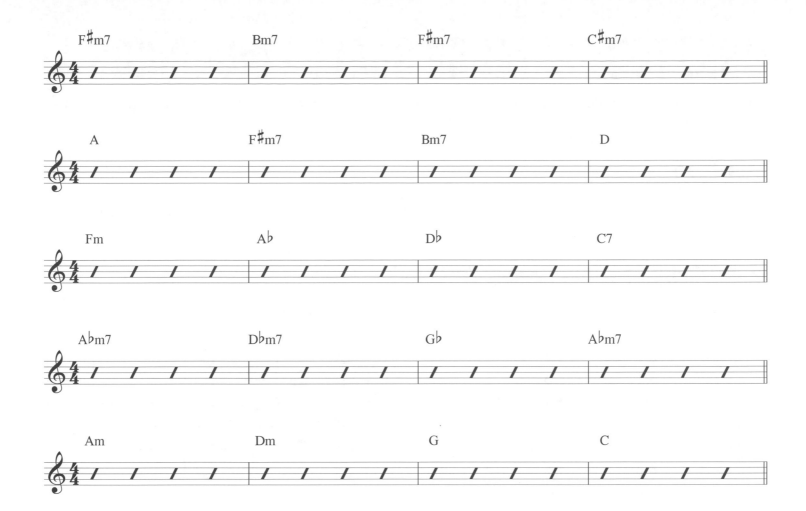

CHAPTER 12: MORE SCALE FINGERINGS

This section shows fingerings for all major/relative minor, melodic minor, harmonic minor, and pentatonic/blues scales from frets 5–9.

Exercises

Apply the patterns shown in Chapter 5 to the major and minor scales here. Apply the patterns from Chapter 6 to the pentatonic and blues scales, respectively. (The major roots are indicated with an open square while the minor roots are indicated with a filled square.)

Major/Relative Minor Scales: Frets 5–9

A Major/F# Minor

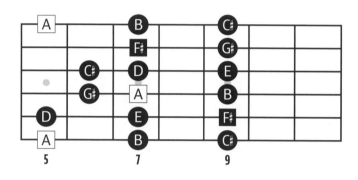

B♭ Major/G Minor

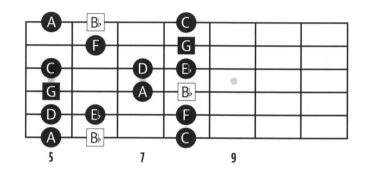

B Major/G# Minor

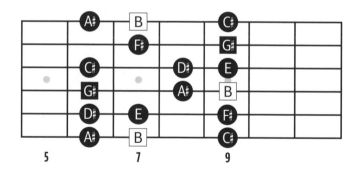

C Major/A Minor

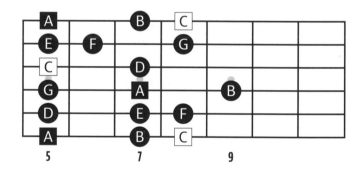

D♭ Major/B♭ Minor

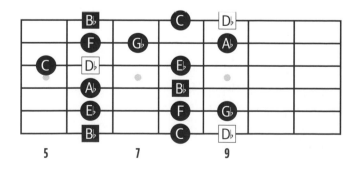

D Major/B Minor

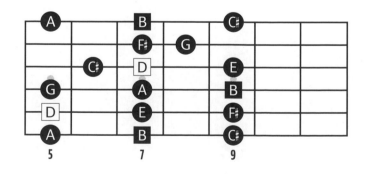

E♭ Major/C Minor

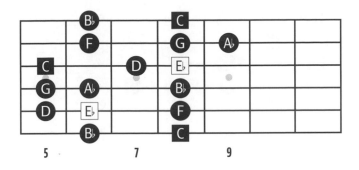

E Major/C♯ Minor

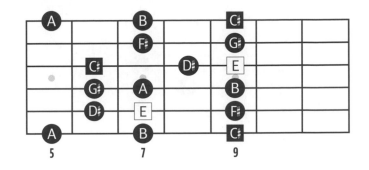

F Major/D Minor

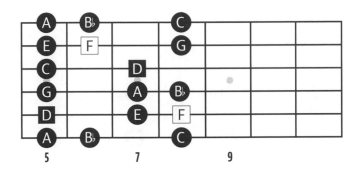

G♭ Major/E♭ Minor

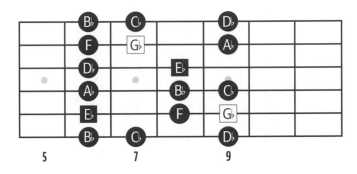

G Major/E Minor

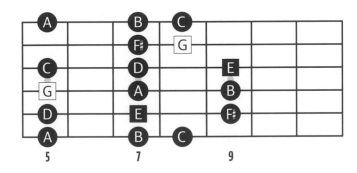

A♭ Major/F Minor

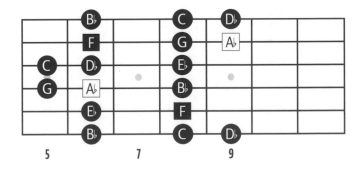

Melodic Minor Scales: Frets 5–9

A Melodic Minor

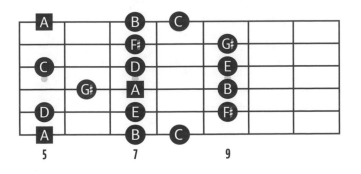

B♭ Melodic Minor

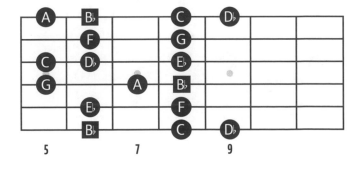

77

B Melodic Minor

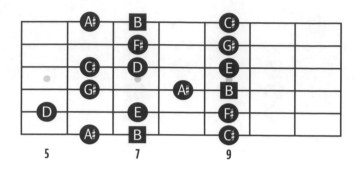

C Melodic Minor

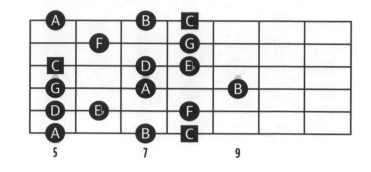

D♭ Melodic Minor

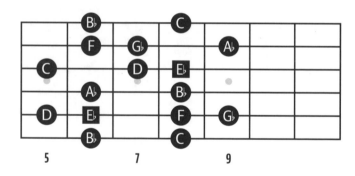

D Melodic Minor

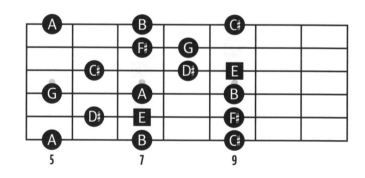

E♭ Melodic Minor

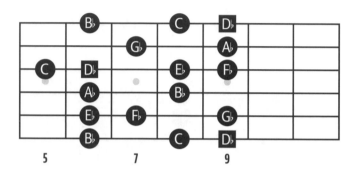

E Melodic Minor

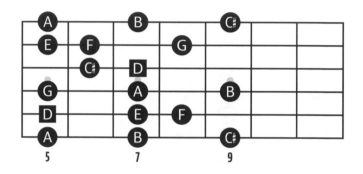

F Melodic Minor

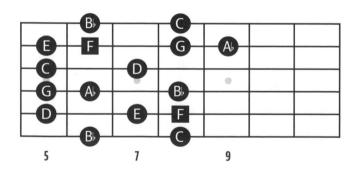

F# Melodic Minor

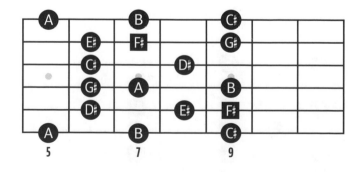

G Melodic Minor

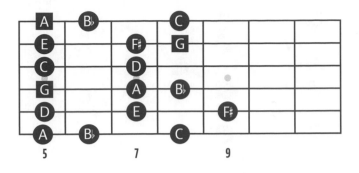

A♭ Melodic Minor

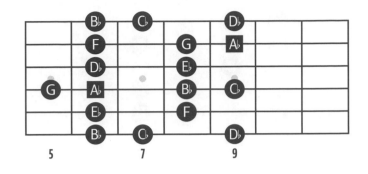

Harmonic Minor Scales: Frets 5–9

A Harmonic Minor

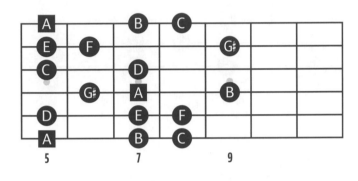

B♭ Harmonic Minor

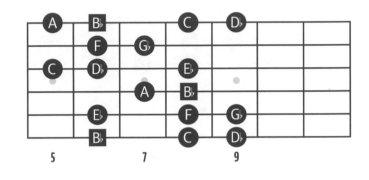

B Harmonic Minor

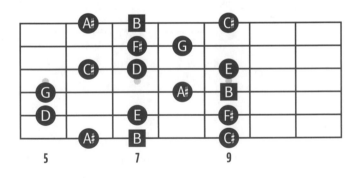

C Harmonic Minor

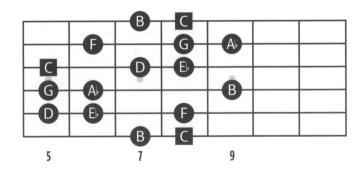

C# Harmonic Minor

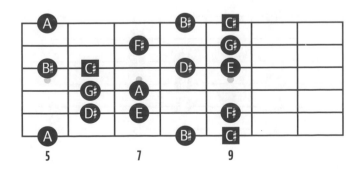

D Harmonic Minor

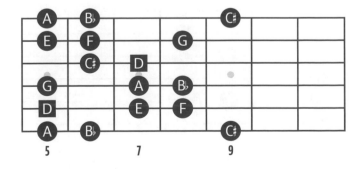

Eb Harmonic Minor

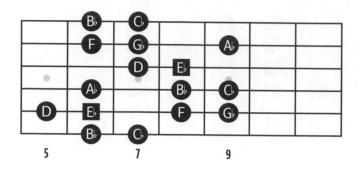

E Harmonic Minor

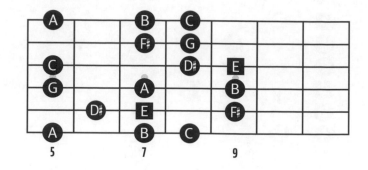

F Harmonic Minor

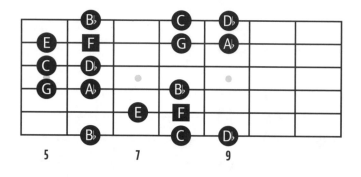

F# Harmonic Minor

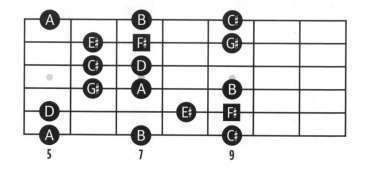

G Harmonic Minor

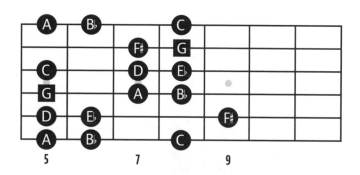

Ab Harmonic Minor

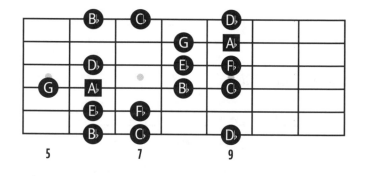

Pentatonic/Blues Scales: Frets 5–9

Each shape here effectively shows a minor pentatonic, major pentatonic, and blues scale. The minor pentatonic root note is shown as a filled square while the relative major tonic note is shown as an open square (for example, A minor and C major), and the blues scale is formed by adding the flatted 5th to the minor pentatonic scale (shown in grey).

A Minor/C Major Pentatonic/Blues

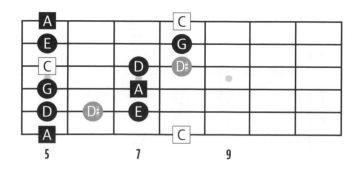

Bb Minor/Db Major Pentatonic/Blues

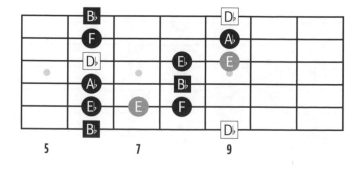

B Minor/D Major Pentatonic/Blues

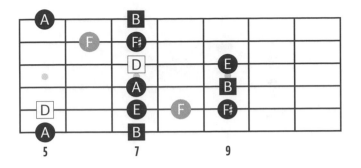

C Minor/E♭ Major Pentatonic/Blues

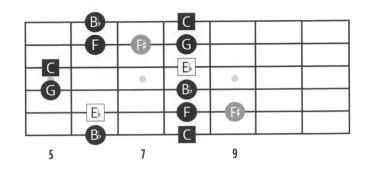

C# Minor/E Major Pentatonic/Blues

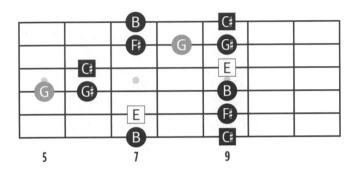

D Minor/F Major Pentatonic/Blues

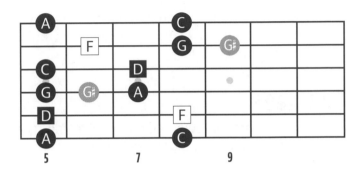

E♭ Minor/G♭ Major Pentatonic/Blues

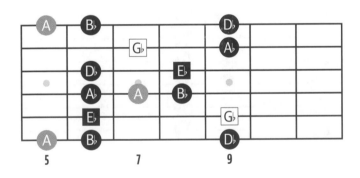

E Minor/G Major Pentatonic/Blues

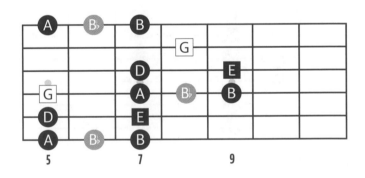

F Minor/A♭ Major Pentatonic/Blues

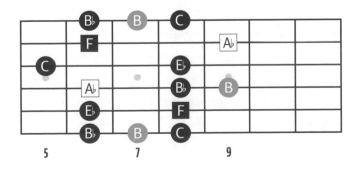

F# Minor/A Major Pentatonic/Blues

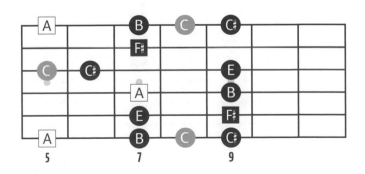

G Minor/B♭ Major Pentatonic/Blues

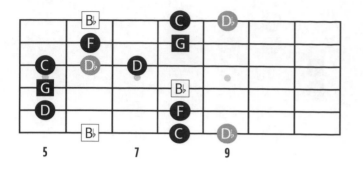

G# Minor/B Major Pentatonic/Blues

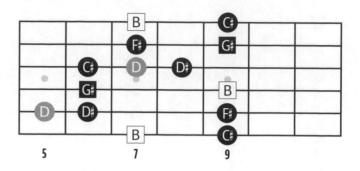

Frets 9–13

This section shows fingerings for all major/relative minor, melodic minor, harmonic minor, and pentatonic/blues scales from frets 9–13. (The major roots are indicated with an open square while the minor roots are indicated with a filled square.)

Exercises

Apply the patterns shown in Chapter 5 to the major and minor scales here. Apply the patterns from Chapters 6 to the pentatonic and blues scales respectively.

Major/Relative Minor Scales: Frets 9–13

D♭ Major/B♭ Minor

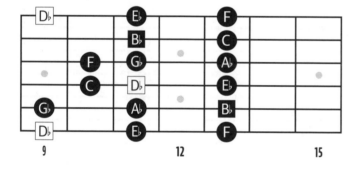

D Major/B Minor

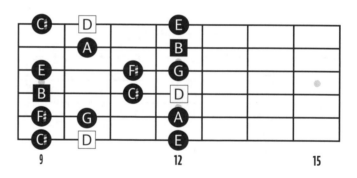

E♭ Major/C Minor

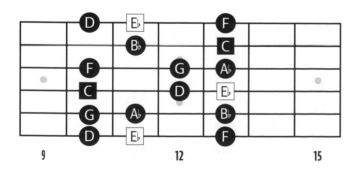

E Major/C# Minor

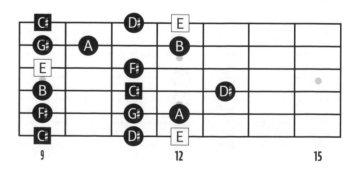

F Major/D Minor

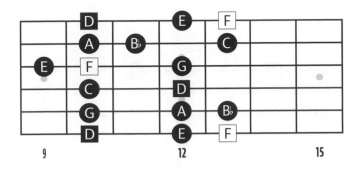

G♭ Major/E♭ Minor

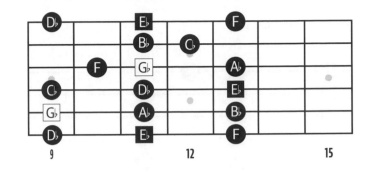

G Major/E Minor

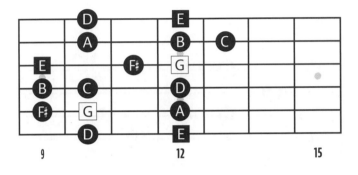

A♭ Major/F Minor

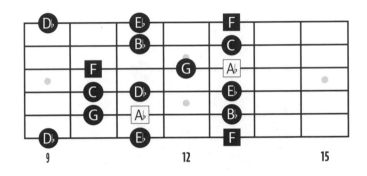

A Major/F♯ Minor

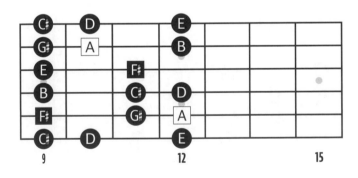

B♭ Major/G Minor

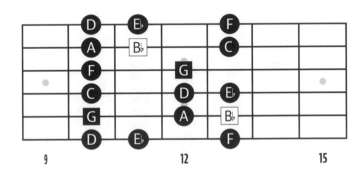

B Major/G♯ Minor

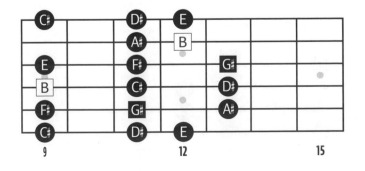

C Major/A Minor

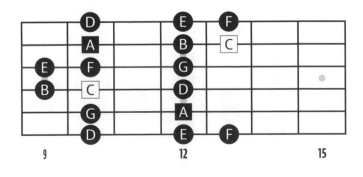

Melodic Minor Scales: Frets 9–13

C# Melodic Minor
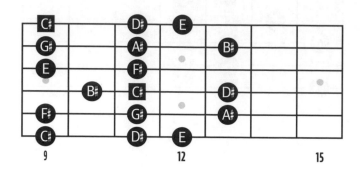

D Melodic Minor
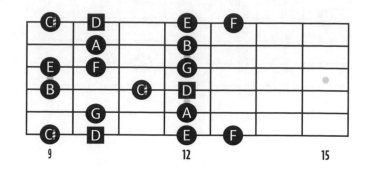

E♭ Melodic Minor
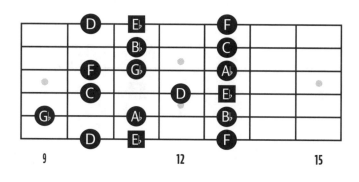

E Melodic Minor
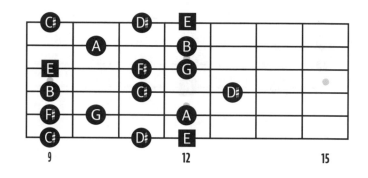

F Melodic Minor
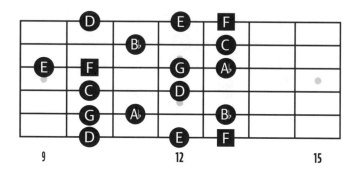

F# Melodic Minor
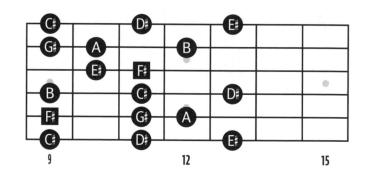

G Melodic Minor
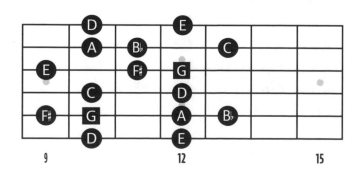

G# Melodic Minor
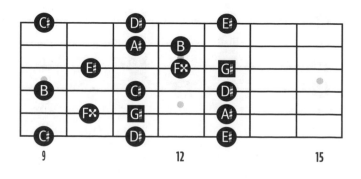

A Melodic Minor

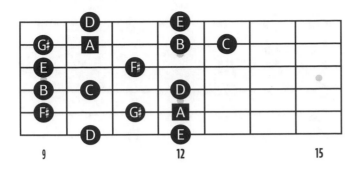

B♭ Melodic Minor

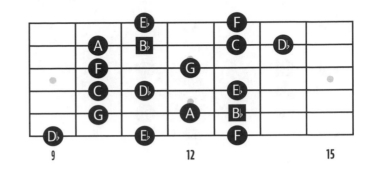

B Melodic Minor

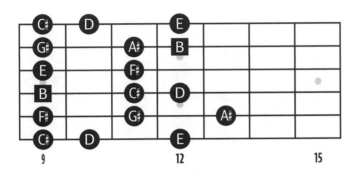

C Melodic Minor

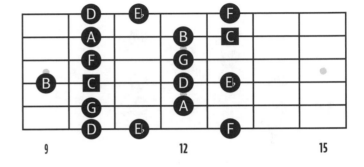

Harmonic Minor Scales: Frets 9–13

C# Harmonic Minor

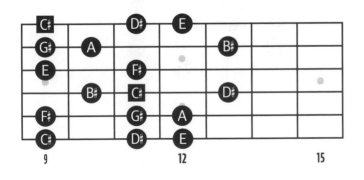

D Harmonic Minor

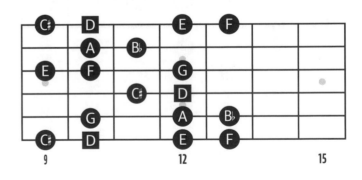

E♭ Harmonic Minor

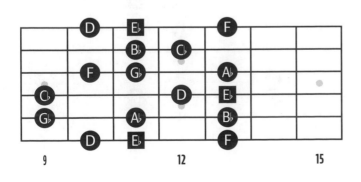

E Harmonic Minor

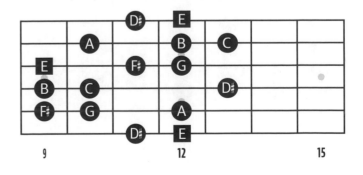

85

F Harmonic Minor

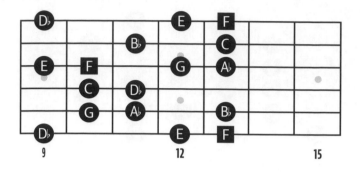

F# Harmonic Minor

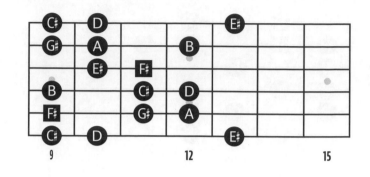

G Harmonic Minor

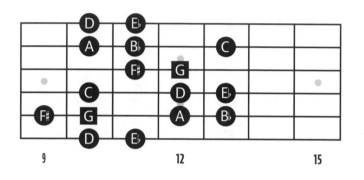

G# Harmonic Minor

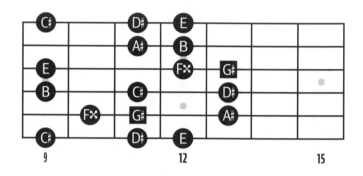

A Harmonic Minor

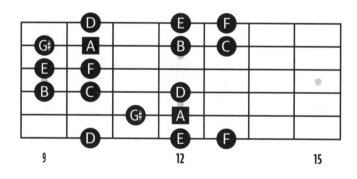

Bb Harmonic Minor

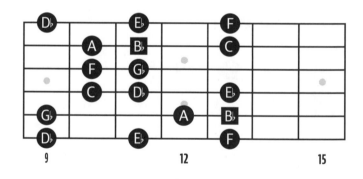

B Harmonic Minor

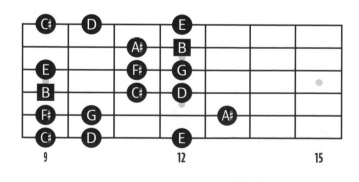

C Harmonic Minor

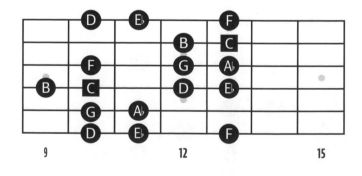

Pentatonic/Blues Scales: Frets 9–13

C# Minor/E Major Pentatonic/Blues

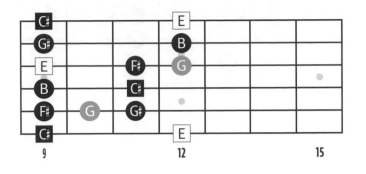

D Minor/F Major Pentatonic/Blues

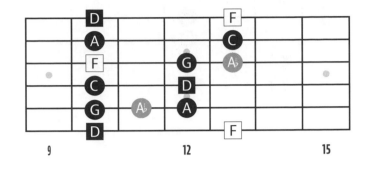

E♭ Minor/G♭ Major Pentatonic/Blues

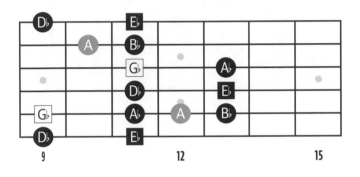

E Minor/G Major Pentatonic/Blues

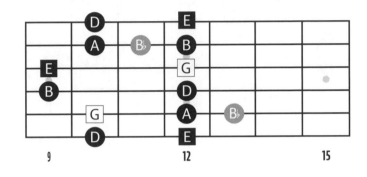

F Minor/A♭ Major Pentatonic/Blues

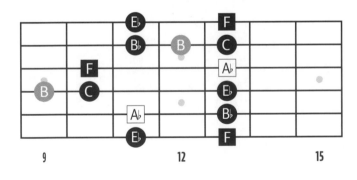

F# Minor/A Major Pentatonic/Blues

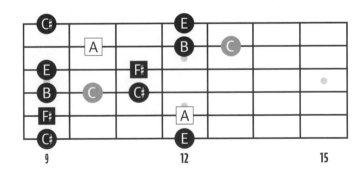

G Minor/B♭ Major Pentatonic/Blues

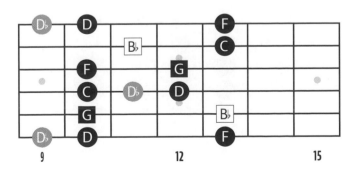

G# Minor/B Major Pentatonic/Blues

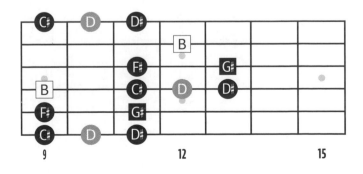

A Minor/C Major Pentatonic/Blues

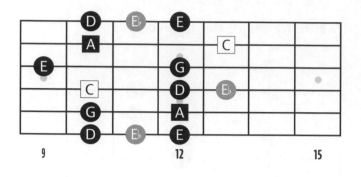

B♭ Minor/D♭ Major Pentatonic/Blues

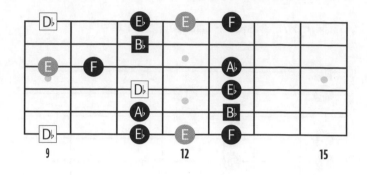

B Minor/D Major Pentatonic/Blues

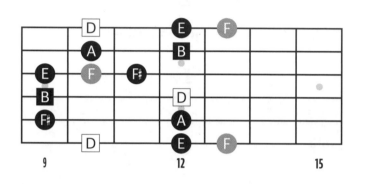

C Minor/E♭ Major Pentatonic/Blues

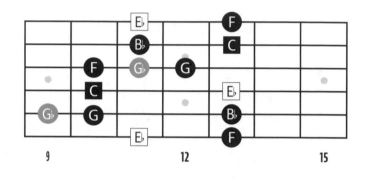

CHAPTER 13: JOINING THE DOTS WITH FRETBOARD MAPPING

Having absorbed the complete set of major scales in three discrete fretboard areas (1–5, 5–9, 9–13), we can begin to put them together and find the notes of any scale or key all over the fretboard.

Beyond the 12th Fret

As there are 12 half steps in an octave, the 12th fret on any given string has the same name as the open string, and note names repeat from here on. (The 13th fret is one octave above the first fret and so on.)

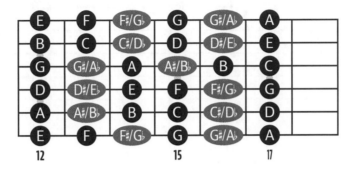

The fret maps and exercises in this chapter stop at the 15th fret, but they can ultimately be applied as far as your fretboard and fingers will allow. (The major roots are shown as an open square while minor roots are shown as a filled square.)

Fretboard Maps: Major/Relative Minor

F Major/D Minor

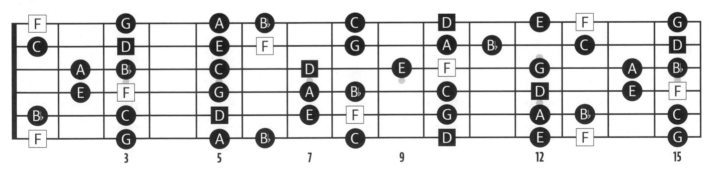

G♭ Major/E♭ Minor

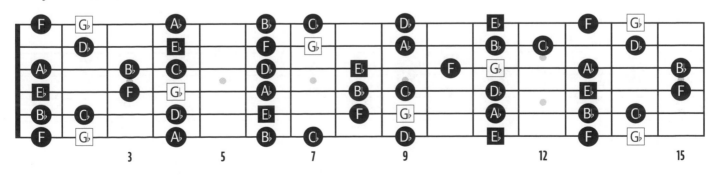

G Major/E Minor

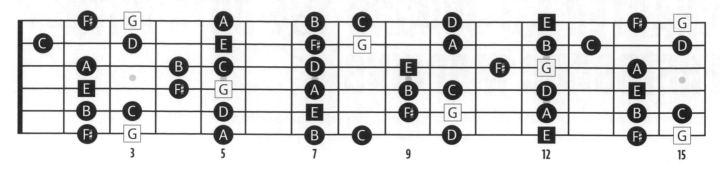

A♭ Major/F Minor

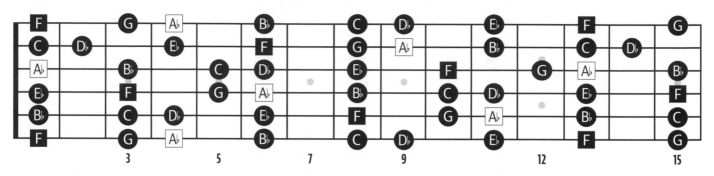

A Major/F♯ Minor

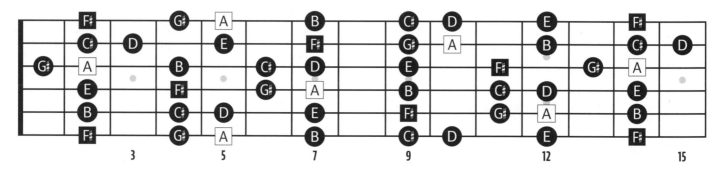

B♭ Major/G Minor

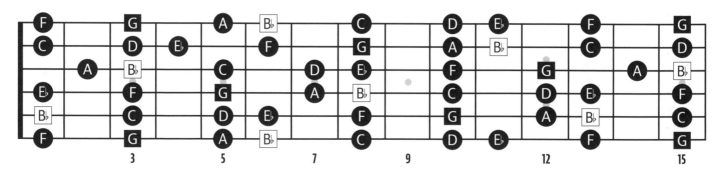

B Major/G♯ Minor

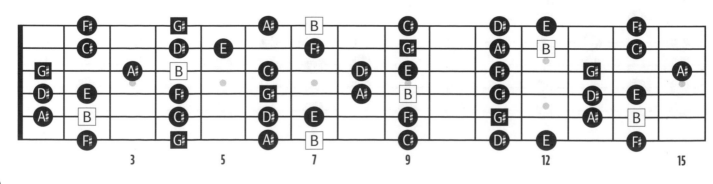

90

C Major/A Minor

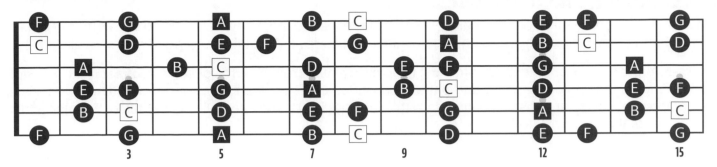

D♭ Major/B♭ Minor

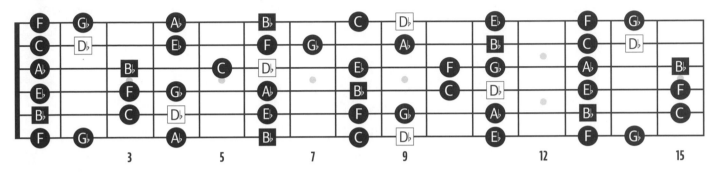

D Major/B Minor

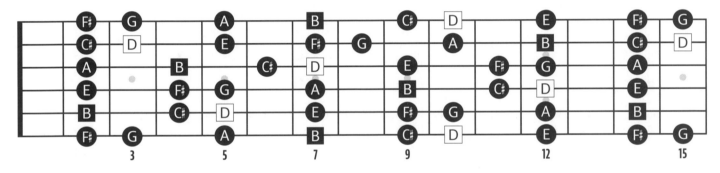

E♭ Major/C Minor

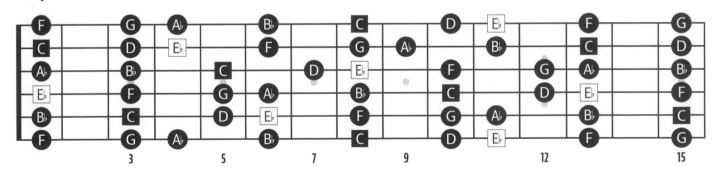

E Major/C♯ Minor

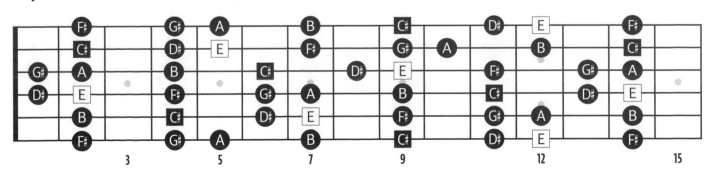

91

Fretboard Chunks and Modes

Producing a fretboard map for any scale allows us to proceed to the next level of fretboard memorization. We can now join each position together and zoom into a greater level of detail at any point on the neck.

Taking F major as an example: Within the first five frets, we can play the F major scale as presented in Chapter 5, including ascending/descending and pattern-based ideas. Then, we can move the first finger to the next step of the scale and transpose all of this up within the key. This helps internalize the notes of F major within a new chunk of the fretboard (frets 3–7).

Though it's not our main focus here, it does no harm to note that these scale inversions are known as the **modes** of the major scale. Any major scale has six related modes, which are essentially scales sharing the same set of notes but with a different key center or tonic note. For example, if we play the notes of F major but with a key center of G, then we produce the second mode of the major scale, also known as the **Dorian** mode. Each mode has a musical flavor of its own. Modes can be numbered in terms of their relation to a parent major scale.

I	Ionian (Major)
II	Dorian
III	Phrygian
IV	Lydian
V	Mixolydian
VI	Aeolian
VII	Locrian

More Exercises

The exercises on the following pages apply the routine described above to two different keys: F major and B major. Instead of leading from the first finger, the B-major exercise leads from the fourth finger. The possibilities are almost limitless in this respect; for a totally comprehensive approach, all scales could be practiced starting with any of the shapes encountered in Chapter 5.

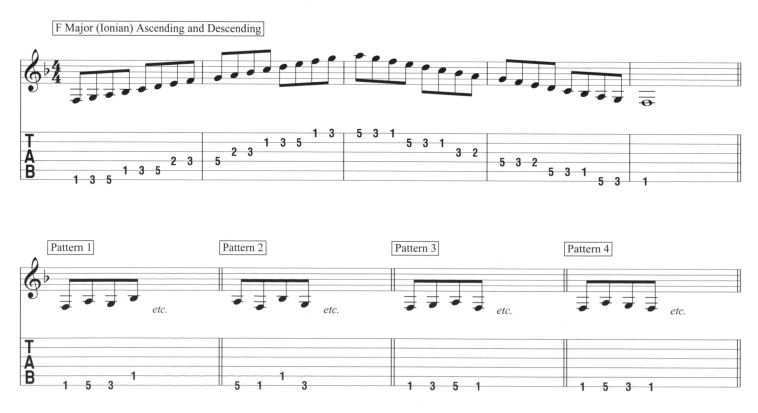

92

(Dorian) Ascending and Descending

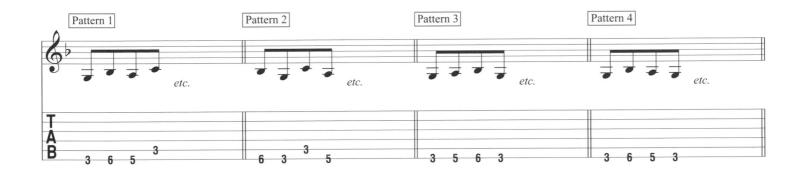

Pattern 1   Pattern 2   Pattern 3   Pattern 4

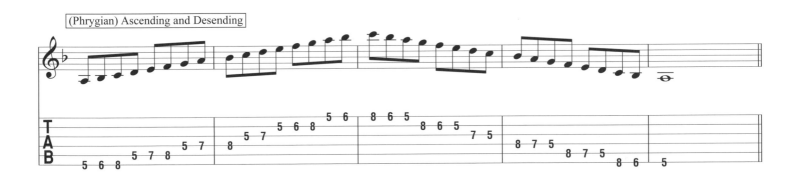

(Phrygian) Ascending and Desending

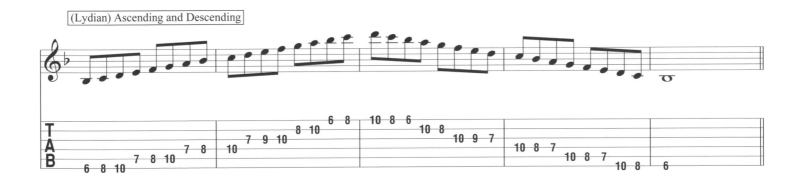

(Lydian) Ascending and Descending

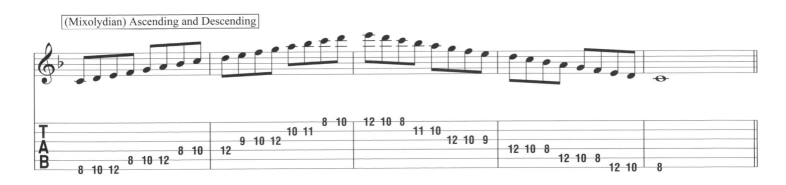

(Mixolydian) Ascending and Descending

(Aeolian) Acsending and Descending

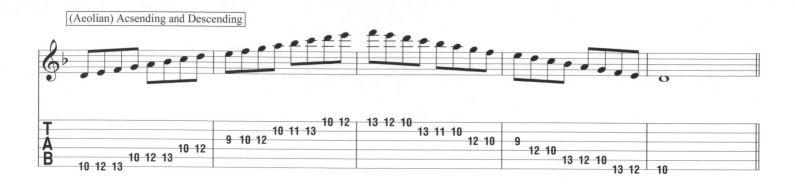

(Locrian) Ascending and Descending

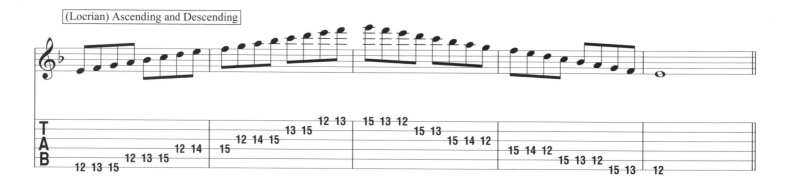

B Major (Ionian) Ascending and Descending

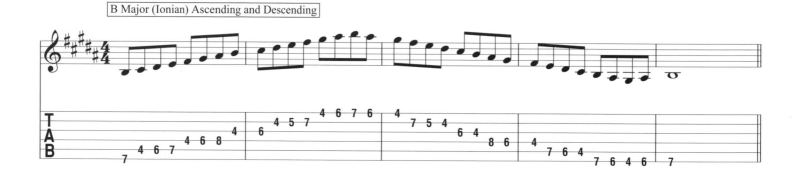

Pattern 1   Pattern 2   Pattern 3   Pattern 4

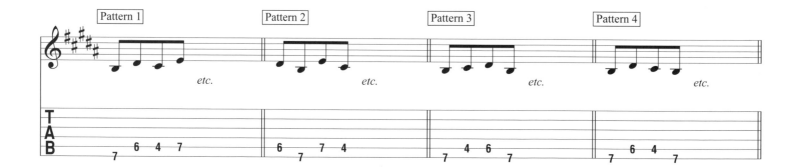

etc.   *etc.*   *etc.*   *etc.*

(Dorian) Ascending and Descending

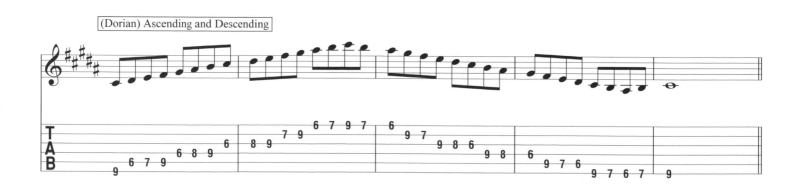

94

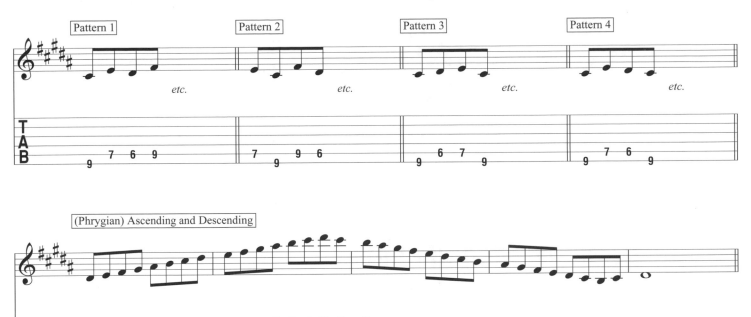

Pattern 1   Pattern 2   Pattern 3   Pattern 4

etc.   *etc.*   *etc.*   *etc.*

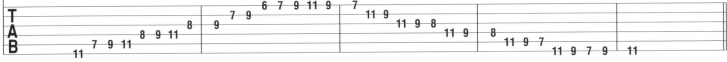

(Phrygian) Ascending and Descending

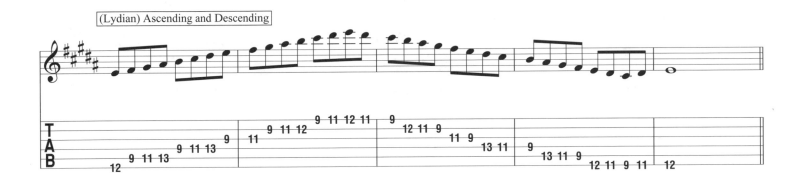

(Lydian) Ascending and Descending

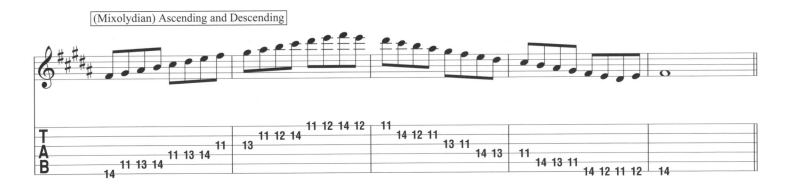

(Mixolydian) Ascending and Descending

(Aeolian) Ascending and Descending

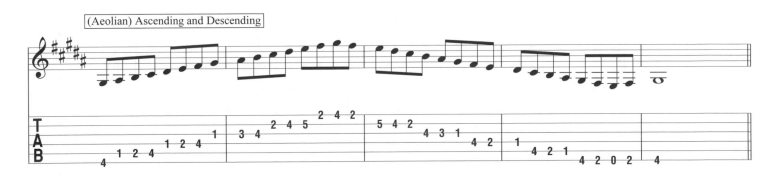

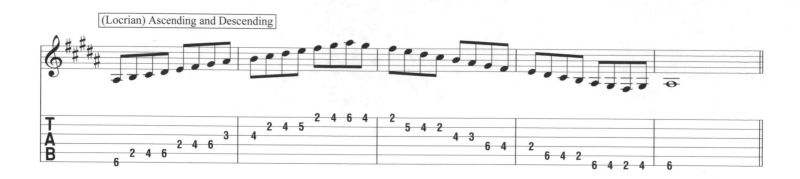

(Locrian) Ascending and Descending

Fretboard Maps: Melodic Minor

To internalize all the notes of each scale, apply the patterns and scale inversions as outlined earlier.

F Melodic Minor

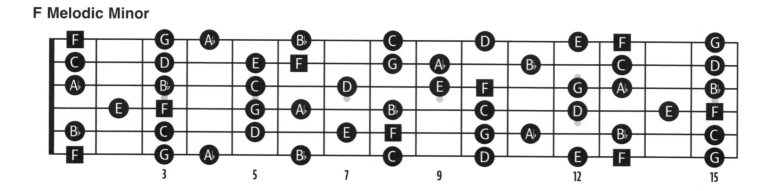

F# Melodic Minor

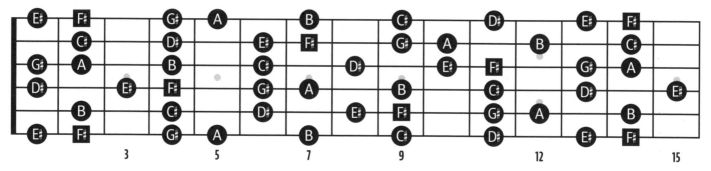

G Melodic Minor

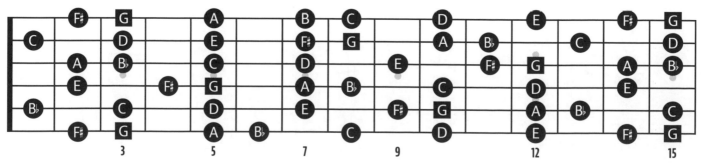

G# Melodic Minor

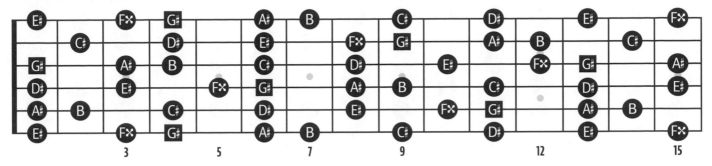

A Melodic Minor

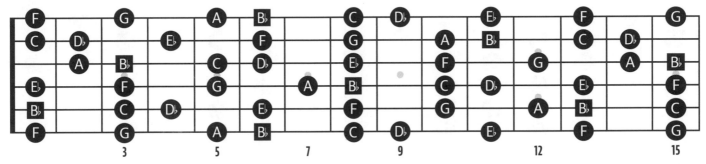

Bb Melodic Minor

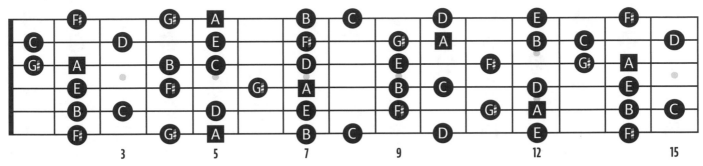

B Melodic Minor

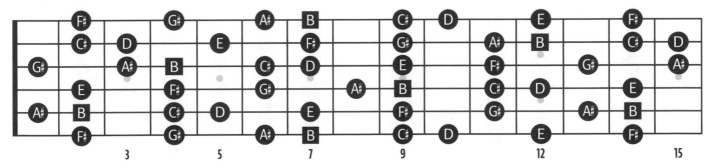

C Melodic Minor

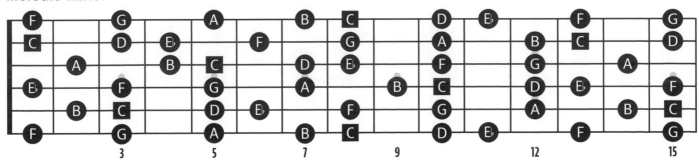

C# Melodic Minor

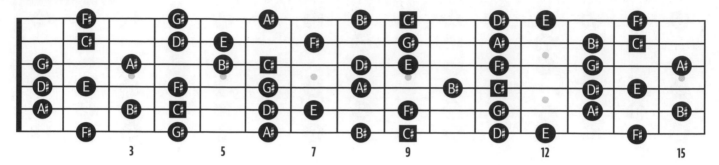

D Melodic Minor

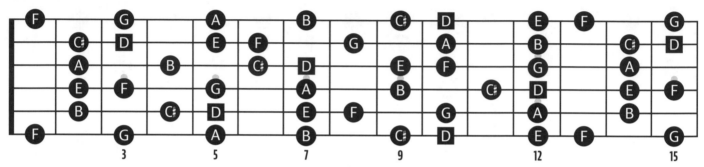

E♭ Melodic Minor

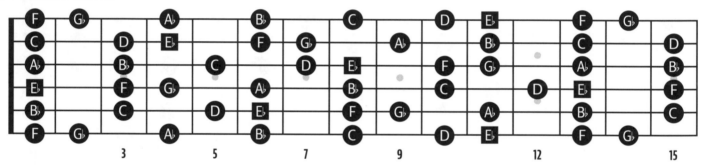

E Melodic Minor

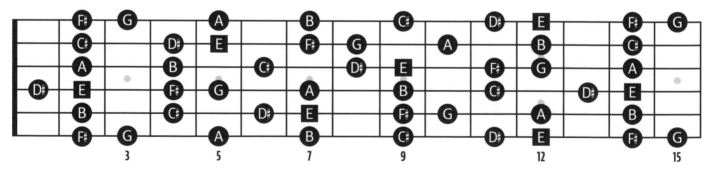

Fretboard Maps: Harmonic Minor

To internalize all the notes of each scale, apply the patterns and scale inversions as outlined earlier in this chapter.

F Harmonic Minor

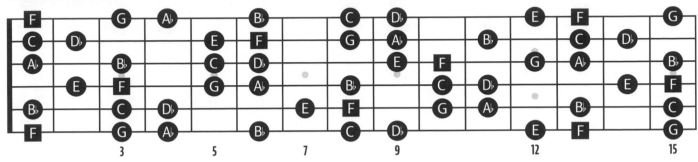

F# Harmonic Minor

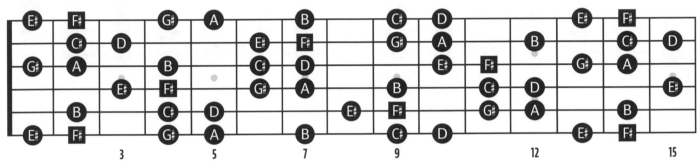

G Harmonic Minor

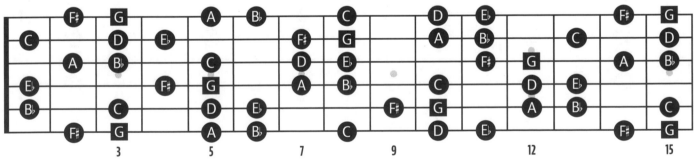

G# Harmonic Minor

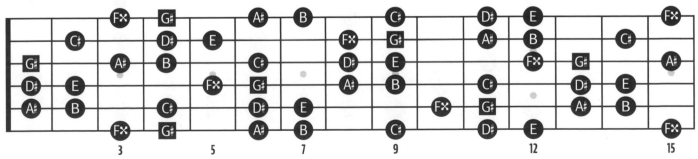

A Harmonic Minor

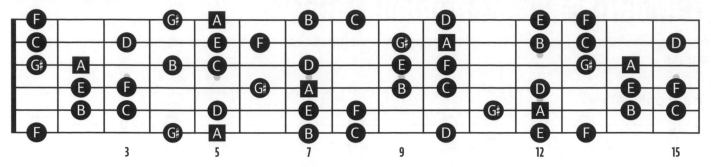

B♭ Harmonic Minor

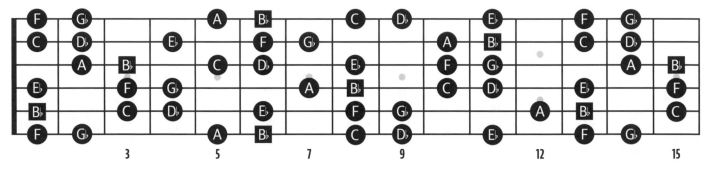

B Harmonic Minor

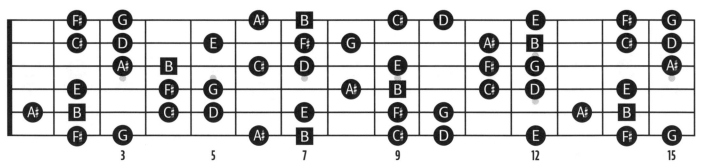

C Harmonic Minor

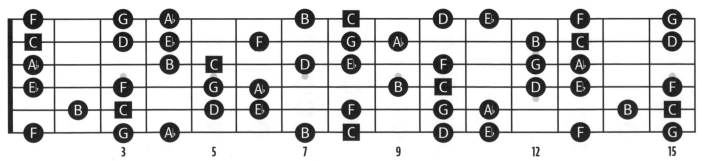

C# Harmonic Minor

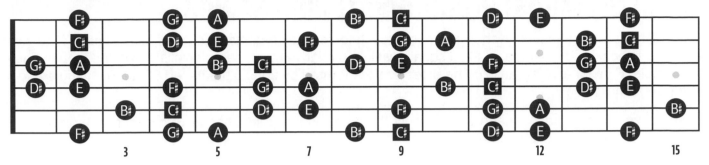

D Harmonic Minor

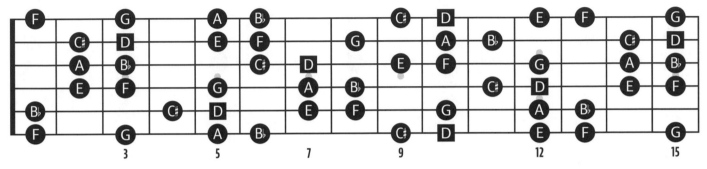

E♭ Harmonic Minor

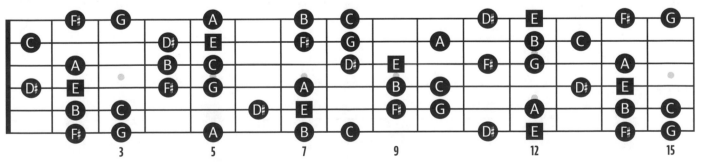

E Harmonic Minor

Fretboard Maps: Pentatonic/Blues Scales

Each fret map here effectively shows a minor pentatonic, major pentatonic, and blues scale. The minor pentatonic tonic note is shown as a filled square while the relative major pentatonic is shown as a open square (for example, F minor and A♭ major). The blues scale is formed by adding the flatted 5th (shown in grey) to the minor pentatonic scale.

To internalize all the notes of each scale, apply the patterns found in Chapter 6, moving through the scale inversions as outlined in this chapter.

F Minor/A♭ Major

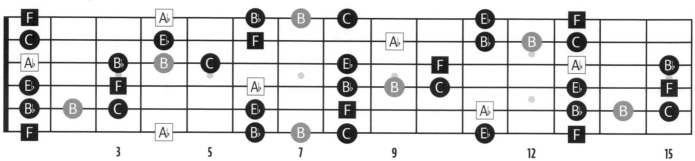

F♯ Minor/A Major

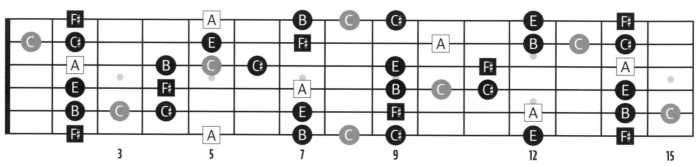

G Minor/B♭ Major

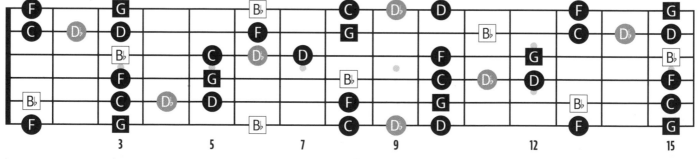

G♯ Minor/B Major

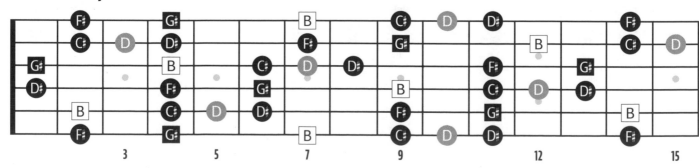

A Minor/C Major

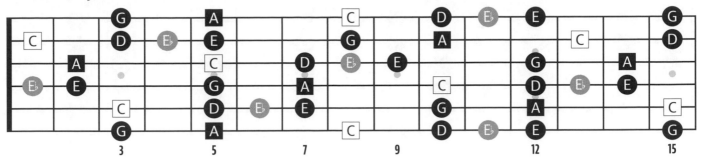

B♭ Minor/D♭ Major

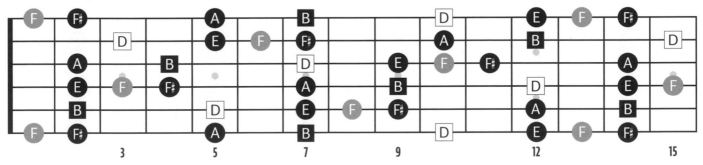

B Minor/D Major

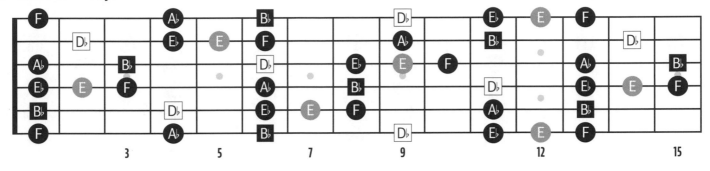

C Minor/E♭ Major

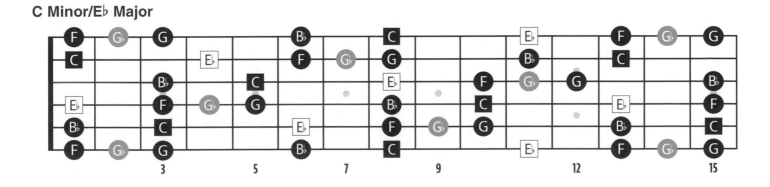

C# Minor/E Major

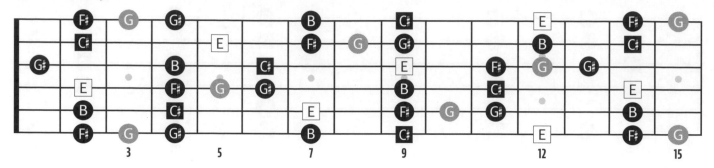

D Minor/F Major

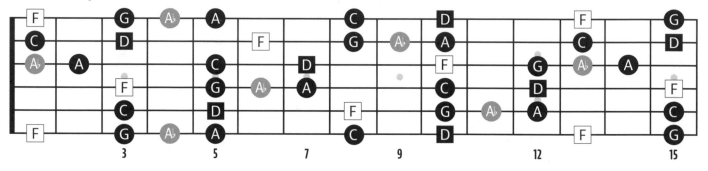

E♭ Minor/G♭ Major

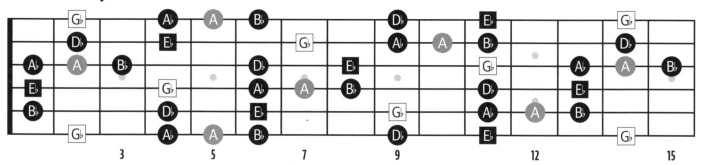

E Minor/G Major

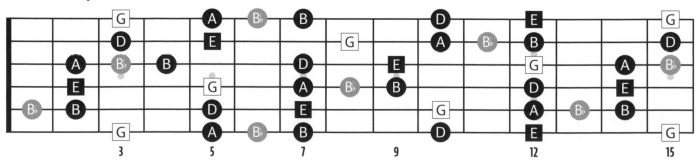